The God Who Comforts

The God Who Comforts

A Forty-Day Meditation on John 14:1—16:15

Douglas D. Webster

CASCADE *Books* • Eugene, Oregon

THE GOD WHO COMFORTS
A Forty-Day Meditation on John 14:1—16:15

Cascade Books
An Imprint of Wipf and Stock Publishers
199 W. 8th Ave., Suite 3
Eugene, OR 97401

www.wipfandstock.com

ISBN 13: 978-1-4982-3440-5

Cataloguing-in-Publication Data

Webster, Douglas D.

    The God who comforts : a forty-day meditation on John 14:1—16:15 /
Douglas D. Webster.

    xii + 150 p. ; 23 cm. Includes bibliographical references.

    ISBN 13: 978-1-4982-3440-5

    1. Bible, John commentaries. 2. Pastoral theology. I. Title.

BS2615.2.W43 2016

Manufactured in the USA.   01/06/2016

Jim Johnson
a paraclete for Central Presbyterian Church

Contents

Contents

Comfort and Challenge

DISCIPLES EVERYWHERE AND IN every generation explore in depth Jesus' discipleship sermon. The upper room experience deserves a close reading of the text—a *lectio divina* (divine reading). We began with a forty day meditation in John 13 entitled *The God Who Kneels*. This earlier work focused on the sacrificial continuum from foot-washing to cross-bearing, and explored how the towel and the basin, the bread and the cup, are emblematic of the divine atonement and the praxis of discipleship. Jesus' last redemptive parable, washing the disciples' feet, and his new commandment mandate to love one another "as I have loved you," sets forth what it means to follow Jesus until he comes again. Jesus supplies all the action in John 13. He disrobed, knelt, and washed the disciples' feet. Then he robed and returned to his place to teach. At the table, his coming and going is confined to hosting and serving. All the while Jesus instructed his disciples on what it means to follow him.

In the upper room questions were asked, body language read, and understanding was sealed with a nod. The setting was intimate. Jesus' spiritual direction was conversational. Face-to-face dialogue encouraged a dynamic interplay between the personal and conceptual. Jesus encouraged the disciples to go deeper into the hope of his real presence and into the challenge of his real obedience. What started out as a Passover meal together became an inspiring and spiraling manifesto of comfort and challenge. Jesus propels the conversation forward into our hearts and minds.

A prayerful reading of John 14 and 16 reveals an eschatological focus to our Lord's discipleship sermon. Jesus frames the meaning of discipleship in the big picture of his multiple comings, four in all.

Jesus begins with his ultimate coming: "I will come again and take you to be with me that you also may be where I am" (14:3). This final coming is preceded by his resurrection coming: "I will not leave you as orphans; I will come to you. Before long, the world will not see me anymore, but you will see me. Because I live, you also will live" (14:18–19). His resurrection coming makes possible the coming of the Holy Spirit (14:26). "When the Advocate comes, whom I will send to you from the Father—the Spirit of Truth who goes out from the Father—he will testify about me" (15:26). But embedded in these other comings is the immediacy of his continuous homecoming. "Remain in me, as I also remain in you" (15:4).

These four comings, the Parousia, the Passion, the Paraclete, and his abiding Presence, reveal the true nature of the comfort and challenge of God. They define the meaning of human flourishing and the path of human destiny. When Jesus got up off his knees and resumed his place of authority, he framed this strategic discourse in the truth that cannot be packaged as a consumer product or programmed to fit the secular mind. The soul's real comfort depends upon the comings and goings of Jesus, who is one with the Father, the sender of the Spirit, and the returning King.

John captures the poetic, passionate, and practical impact of Jesus' meditations on discipleship in the upper room. Maybe this is why these verses have been memorized by so many believers for both comfort and challenge. If we are willing to hear what the master has to say, Jesus' discourse in John 14–16 promises to resonate with our souls and change our lives. His words are accessible to new believers and inexhaustible to mature believers. Ignatius of Loyola, founder of the Jesuits and author of *The Spiritual Exercises* (1548), offered this counsel for our upper room reflection:

> It is not the quantity of food, but a healthy digestion, which nourishes the body; so it is not the great amount of knowledge communicated, but the manner in which the heart receives it, and is nourished by it, that satisfies the needs of the soul. Moreover, experience proves that the heart will receive with delight, and with greater

real profit, what it discovers for itself, either by its own reflections, or by the light shed upon it by Divine grace, than what is presented to its intelligence by lengthened discourses.[1]

1. Ignatius of Loyola, *The Spiritual Exercises*, 3.

DAY 1

Nobody Knows the Trouble I've Seen

"Do not let your hearts be troubled."

John 14:1

IN HIS MEMORABLE VOICE, Louis Armstrong intones the old spiritual,

> Nobody knows the trouble I've seen; nobody knows my
> sorrows.
> Nobody knows the trouble I've seen. Glory Hallelujah.
> Sometimes I'm up; sometimes I'm down. Oh, yes, Lord.
> Sometimes I'm almost to the ground. Oh, yes, Lord.
> Nobody knows the trouble I've seen;
> Nobody knows, but Jesus.
> Nobody knows the trouble I've seen. Glory Hallelujah.

Trouble is an inescapable fact of life. As one of Job's unfriendly friends famously said, "Yet man is born to trouble as surely as sparks fly upward" (Job 5:7). Trouble is universal and pervasive. It touches all of our lives deeply and personally. Each of us seems to have our own original experience of trouble that no one else can share. We agree: "nobody knows the trouble I've seen." We cherish the lament that is uniquely our own. Trouble is trouble, but nobody knows the trouble I've seen; nobody knows *my* sorrows.

"Let not your hearts be troubled," is often said at funerals to comfort the bereaved with the hope of heaven, for "in my Father's house are many rooms." This comforting one-liner is lifted from Jesus' upper room discourse as a healing salve for the grief at hand. But Jesus' imperative was directed to his disciples who were troubled by news of his departure and disturbed by his forewarning of betrayal and denial. They found Jesus' line of reasoning deeply troubling. His cruciform conversation ran counter to the kind of troubles they might have anticipated in their hopeful vision of Jesus' social impact. Yet the particular meaning of trouble that Jesus had in mind was specifically tied to following him and the Good Friday reality. Generic trouble was not the object of Jesus' imperative. It was the costly sacrifice of the cross that the disciples found so troubling.

I have African American friends who insist that I will never know the trouble they've seen. They may be right. But at some point all our troubles, those that are shared and those that are not, are eclipsed by the cross of Christ. Prioritizing our troubles under the cross and disciplining our hearts to seek the peace of Christ is vastly different from the untroubled heart that has never embraced the claims of Christ. Complacency needs no comfort. We can throw up a smoke screen of troubles that makes it impossible to understand what Jesus meant when he said, "Do not let your hearts be troubled."

Twice we are told that Jesus was troubled. Just days before, after Jesus had predicted his death and outlined the costly path of discipleship, he said, "Now my soul is troubled, and what shall I say? 'Father, save me from this hour'? No, it was for this very reason I came to this hour. Father, glorify your name!" (John 12:27–28). And then again in the upper room after he predicted his betrayal, John reports that Jesus "was troubled in spirit and testified, 'Very truly I tell you, one of you is going to betray me'" (John 13:21).

He who was deeply troubled, and only hours away from the soul-wrenching experience of Gethsemane, commands his followers, "Do not let your hearts be troubled." The explanation for this paradox can be found in Jesus' capacity to do for us what we cannot do for ourselves. He experienced trouble for us so we might live trouble-free in the most profound sense ever imagined ("the punishment that brought us peace was on him and by his wounds we are healed" (Isa 53:5]).

All who truly follow the Lord Jesus acquire over time a capacity to absorb this trouble for the sake of others. Even though their souls may be deeply troubled, they echo their Lord's imperative, "Do not let your hearts be troubled," to their children and friends. Pastors, parents, and friends offer this spiritual direction to those under their responsibility in a manner reminiscent of Jesus in the upper room. Many years after the fact, I realize now my mother's extraordinary capacity to absorb trouble for our family. She was the principle caregiver, first for me and my cancer surgery, and then for my dad who died from cancer. This trouble was followed by the death of my grandparents and aunt, all of whom depended upon my mother for sole support and comfort. Through it all, she courageously lived out her Resurrection Hope and heeded the Lord's admonition, "Let not your hearts be troubled. You believe in God; believe also in me." The late Andrae Crouch expressed it well, when he sang, "Through it all, through it all, I've learned to trust in Jesus, I've learned to trust in God. Through it all, through it all, I've learned to depend upon His Word."

Upper Room Reflection

How would you define the trouble Jesus had in mind?

Who is the best person to offer this admonition to you?

Have you echoed this command to others?

How can you absorb cruciform trouble and commend Jesus' spiritual imperative to others?

DAY 2

So, Who Can You Trust?

"Believe in God; believe also in me."

John 14:1

WE HAVE ALL HEARD stories of unbelievers who have rejected Christ because of unreliable Christians. I'm sure it's true that if we disciples were more faithful, our evangelism would be more fruitful. Sadly, the corporate testimony of the church fits the upper room profile of weak and fallible disciples. They were bickering and debating about who was the greatest (Luke 22:24), bewildered by Jesus' warning of a betrayer, and confused by his spiritual direction. They were overconfident and unreliable, yet they prided themselves on their courage and loyalty. The upper room testifies that faith's foundation cannot rest on others no matter who they are.

Our only hope is clearly stated: "Believe in God; believe also in me." Only then is the trust factor commensurate with the trouble we face and the trouble in us. This is because we need the redemption that only God can provide. We may want a good therapist or life coach to advise us on how to manage life and focus our emotions. We may think, "If I only had a better job or a little more income, I'd have it made." But the trouble is deeper and more fundamental than we realize. No amount of adjustments or affirmation removes the need for atonement. The antidote to deep trouble is real trust in God.

The simple phrase, "Trust in God; trust also me," particularizes and personalizes the foundation of faith in Jesus himself.

Familiarity with the biblical text can obscure the boldness of the truth proclaimed here: God and Jesus are one. If these words are heard with Muslim ears or Jewish ears they deliver a shock. The truth of the gospel is scandalous. It is precisely because we are such failed and flawed creatures that the normal person knows he cannot be the object of faith and trust. Yet this is what Jesus boldly claimed. We can't forgive sins and give people hope. We can't calm storms and heal diseases. But Jesus can.

The famous American preacher Harry Emerson Fosdick was by all accounts a remarkable man, gracious, winsome, approachable, and personable. He modernized the biblical Jesus, making him accessible to thousands, through sermons that touched the heart and the mind. He believed in the historical Jesus, which is to say, he believed in the humanity of Jesus. But Fosdick did not believe that Jesus was God incarnate. Jesus lived his life open to God in the most exemplary way and gave his disciples a truly human experience of God. But Jesus was not in his very essence God or born of the virgin Mary. This is why Fosdick refused to confess the Apostles' Creed and denied the bodily resurrection of Christ. For Fosdick, talk of the real incarnation or the substitutionary atonement was a poetic or mythical way to describe Jesus' human importance and spiritual impact.

U2's front man Bono was asked, "What or who is Jesus?" He replied, "He went around claiming to be the Messiah, the Son of God, that is why he was crucified. He was crucified because he said he was the Son of God. So either he was the Son of God or he was . . ." and the interviewer interrupted, finishing Bono's thought with "not." But Bono shot back, "No, no, no, he was nuts. Forget rock and roll messianic complexes, its more like Charles Manson delirium." "So," the interviewer asked, "therefore it follows that you believe that Jesus was divine and rose from the dead physically?" Bono, "Yes. I have no problem with miracles. I'm living around them. I am one."[1]

---

1. Bono, "On faith and Jesus," www.youtube.com/watch?v=Vlm7JRSo6w4.

THE GOD WHO COMFORTS

"Do you believe in God?" Jesus asks. "Then believe also in me; for you can only believe in God through me!"[2] Earlier in the Gospel Jesus said that faith in him was the basis for faith in God (John 5:38; 8:46–48), now he is saying that faith in God is the basis for trusting in him. The truth runs in either direction. If you believe in Jesus, you believe in God; and if you believe in God, you believe in Jesus. Jesus has more to say about his relationship with the Father, but we know now that we can't know God apart from Jesus and to know Jesus is to know God.

Jesus said this in the upper room just before it became very difficult for the disciples to believe in him. He is headed to the cross. He appears to be the unreliable one. He comes off looking like the loser, who fails to capitalize on his popularity and make something of his movement. He submits to the religious and political forces without a fight. No wonder the disciples scattered. Their denial and abandonment of Jesus was the natural outcome of Jesus' failure to succeed. They had not failed Jesus as much as Jesus had failed them. He left them, before they left him. That's how the disciples felt.

If you are looking for an excuse to flee the faith, you can find one in Jesus. The disciples did. The cross is real and remains real. If you want Jesus apart from the cross, as the disciples did and millions of professing believers do, then you will find a ready excuse to scatter when life doesn't go according to plan. If you have ever been tempted to forsake the faith because life took an unexpected turn for the worse, you are in a good place to hear Jesus say, "You believe in God; believe also in me."

2. Bultmann, *The Gospel of John*, 600.

Upper Room Reflection

Have you been tempted to forsake Christ because of other Christians?

Have you even felt that Christ failed you?

What does it mean to you to trust in Jesus?

Are there situations in your life that never seem to get better? How can you trust Christ in these situations?

DAY 3

The Ultimate Homecoming

"My Father's house has many rooms; if that were not so,
would I have told you that I am going there to prepare
a place for you? And if I go and prepare a place for you,
I will come back and take you to be with me that you
also may be where I am."

John 14:2–3

JESUS' PENDING DEPARTURE AND mission are as real as his incarnation and foot-washing. In his farewell discipleship sermon he converges the temporal and eternal dimensions of the most real world. His departure and his work are real and set up our waiting and anticipation. Jesus' final coming frames everything he has to say about salvation, the Holy Spirit, abiding in him, and weathering the world's persecution. Jesus does not elaborate on his work, except to assure us that there will be plenty of room and that he is preparing a place for all those who trust in him.

Jesus sets his three other goings and comings (the Passion, the Paraclete, and the Presence) in the context of his future and final return. The Greek New Testament word used to describe this final coming is *parousia*, which means literally, "presence"—par(a) = "beside," and ousa = "to be," thus parousia = "to be beside." Our future reality is defined best in relationship, not in real estate. "What we call 'heaven,' John's Jesus calls 'where I am.'"[1] His voice (John 5:28–29), his presence (John 12:26, 32), and his desire for us (John 17:24) define our future home. The Father's house is "the real

1. Bruner, *The Gospel of John*, 811.

8

presence of Jesus Christ himself with his people. This is the next life's most simple, compact, intimate, and adequate definition."[2] We best avoid going beyond this description of heaven. I have been to funerals in which the dearly departed are pictured on an eternal spending spree in heaven's shopping mall or playing golf everyday at the celestial country club. To fantasize about heaven in this trivial way indicates that we cannot imagine enjoying the presence of Christ apart from our worldly pleasures. The Father's house is the ultimate homecoming and Jesus makes it possible. Sooner or later we discover that our lasting home is not where we're from, but where we're going.

We come to realize that searching for our true home in God is made difficult by living in a society that seeks to dismantle the connection between heaven and earth. We are a society of restless nomads looking for a little heaven on earth, defining our identity by appearances, insisting on relationships that meet our needs, and then wondering why we suffer from loneliness. Absorbed in our own life stories, we miss the opportunity to become involved in the greater drama of God's salvation history. In our lame attempt to give ourselves purpose, we reject the purpose God intends for us. If we are not careful we can grow accustomed to an endless search for meaning and purpose without ever expecting to find our true home. We can wrap our lives around small pursuits, like shopping or sports, to avoid having to deal with life.

Before our family moved away from Toronto, I wanted to show my sons where I grew up. I wanted them to see my roots. So one day we drove from Toronto to Buffalo, stopping off at Niagara Falls to take some pictures. We visited my parents' first home in Hamburg, New York, and then we visited the cemetery where my father was buried in Orchard Park. The boys posed by the memorial stone of their grandfather, who they never met. Jeremiah and Andrew were good sports that day. We took pictures of my elementary school and high school and our old house in Williamsville.

2. Ibid.

I learned two lessons on that one-day journey. First, home is not so much a place as a family. It is far more personal than an old house or past memories, even though the place and the memories may be very good. My sons were not impressed by my old houses and schools, and I realized in their company that I wasn't very impressed with these places either. Second, I learned that home is not where I'm from, but where I'm going. I had no desire to return to my roots or live in the past. Life moves on and I was caught up in a relational story that was growing and deepening with gospel meaning. No matter how loving and caring our families may be, the search for home will never be satisfied by our immediate family. What we need is to be adopted into God's family. We are born into this world with an identity that drags us down, and that is why we never find our real home until we are adopted into God's family. There is a deeper, more abiding relationship that we were created to experience, which gives meaning and purpose to all other relationships.

My awareness of heaven may lie somewhere between my six-year-old grandson Liam and my father. Five year olds have yet to grasp the strange real world that surrounds them. The line between fantasy and fact blurs even in even the brightest child. I contrast my grandson with his great grandfather who died from cancer at the age of forty-nine. Lying in the hospital bed, my father had been unresponsive for several days. Then, moments before he died, he opened his eyes wide, looked straight at my mother, motioned toward the window, raised both arms up in the air, and died. But for us, it truly felt more like a passing from death to life, than from life to death.

In the Gospel of John, we read, "He was in the world, and though the world was made through him, the world did not recognize him. He came to that which was his own, but his own did not receive him." People regularly fail to recognize who Jesus Christ is. But that need not be said of you or me. We hear the truth proclaimed. We have every opportunity to respond to Christ and embrace his family. The invitation calls for more than an emotional response. Receiving Christ is the primary relationship around which all other relationships revolve. "Yet all who received him, to those who believed in his name, he gave the right to become children of God—born not of natural descent nor of human decision or a husband's will, but born of God" (John 1:10–13).

Upper Room Reflection

Describe your childhood home.

How does the longing for the "Father's house" tame our passion for material success?

What do you expect heaven to be like?

What do you find most comforting about Jesus' words to his disciples?

You Know More than You Know

"You know the way to the place where I am going.
Thomas said to him, 'Lord, we don't know where
you are going, so how can we know the way?'"

John 14:4–5

THOMAS WAS QUICK TO misconstrue Jesus' going-away metaphor. You can sense the impatience in his voice. He had neither the disposition nor the desire to grasp the meaning of Jesus' "representation of the transcendent dwelling of God."[1] He may have been miffed that Jesus was ignoring the real dangers knocking at the door. For Thomas, Jesus' homey and hopeful reference to the Father's house sounded too good to be true. He didn't go for this "pie-in-the-sky" diversion tactic.

The church has plenty of left-brain Thomas-types who insist on nuts and bolts action plans and wooden literalness. They roll their eyes at even minimal theological reflection. I imagine Thomas was more critical of Jesus than he cared to admit. He may have grown cynical. Outside the upper room, the authorities were getting ready to crack down on Jesus and the disciples. Inside, the disciples found Jesus' behavior bewildering. His conversation was a downer. He warned of betrayal, denial, and rejection. Thomas was looking for practical steps to avert disaster and Jesus was talking about heaven. Jesus' words of comfort were not triggering Thomas's praying imagination. You can hear it in his voice. People like

---

1. Beasley-Murray, *John*, 249.

Thomas can be intimidating. They'd prefer to talk about the church budget and building plans than to discuss spiritual growth.

Jesus was patient with Thomas. He calmly persisted with his spiritual direction. "Thank goodness for honest doubting Thomas," writes Dale Bruner, "or we might never have received Jesus' self-definition here, perhaps Jesus' most memorable self-definition in the Gospels."[2] Thomas types can make us better preachers, parents, and friends. Their insistence on not knowing can serve as the catalyst for refining and deepening the message.

Thomas challenged Jesus' straightforward indicative statement: "You know the way to the place where I am going." Had Thomas grown impatient with the master's ambiguity? Was he frustrated with Jesus' oblique references to betrayal. "If you know your betrayer, why not tell us plainly?" Thomas wanted straightforward answers from Jesus. He wanted a definitive action plan laid out step-by-step. Instead, Jesus calmly talked about the future as if he were sitting on a Galilean mountainside. Thomas reminds me of the nuts and bolts church trustee who wants a business plan with a cost-effective analysis. All the while Jesus persisted in leading family devotions.

A church member complained that the reason he never served was because he never was equipped. He had listened to forty years of Bible preaching and had been involved in countless Bible studies, but he lamented that no pastor had ever taken the time to equip him. Like Thomas, he labored under a false perception of practicality. He thought that equipping the saints meant specialized, extra-biblical, how-to instruction. He wanted a step-by-step manual, but what he got was the Bible. The kind of equipping Jesus and the apostles exercised was designed to cultivate the Christian mind, that in turn led to Christian action. The disciples who are equipped are those who allow the Word of God to train and condition them for following Jesus. They have a hunger and thirst for righteousness that is stimulated and satisfied by the Bible. They are salt and light in the midst of decay and darkness. The equipping

2. Bruner, *John*, 811.

process involves an honest, humble teacher who is submissive to the Bible—a person who is capable of communicating its truth effectively and faithfully. This process also involves a sincere, receptive disciple who is ready to do works of service so that the body of Christ may be built up.

Invariably, the people already engaged in ministry get the most out of the Sunday sermon. Those who see themselves as missionaries in the marketplace or Christ's disciples in the classroom take in the preached Word. These salt and light Christians embrace the Word with real joy and practical application.

Thomas knew more than he thought he did. His insistence on a false literalness obscured the truth. Thomas was forgetting Jesus' first principle of the gospel, "Follow me." Like so many of us, Thomas needed "ears to hear" the message of comfort. Jesus framed the present trial in the light of the believer's future hope. The Apostle Paul praised the God of all comfort, "who comforts us in all our troubles, so that we can comfort those in any trouble with the comfort we ourselves received from God" (2 Cor 1:4). If we are going to comfort others we need to receive the message of comfort for ourselves.

Upper Room Reflection

If you had been in the upper room how would you have reacted to Thomas' question?

What was Thomas expecting?

In what ways are you like Thomas?

We cannot give what we have not received.
How do we embrace the message of comfort?

DAY 5

Nobody Knows but Jesus

"I am the way and the truth and the life. No one comes to the Father except through me."

John 14:6

THE SUBJECT WAS TREES and shrubs when the conversation shifted to faith and hope. "I was brought up as a Christian," the landscaper said. "We studied the Bible as a family and went to church every Sunday. Religion was good. It made for a nice life, but I don't have much time for it now. You know, the one thing I can't accept about Christianity, and it really bothers me, is all that business about Jesus being the only way."

We are faced with a critical paradox: the single most comforting and inclusive truth in all the universe is condemned as the most troublesome and exclusionary tenet of the Christian faith. The global village prefers Gandhi's thesis: all religions are true. There is only one transcendent reality and the religions of the world are like blind men describing an elephant. The exclusivity of the gospel is blamed for the appalling intolerance and violence perpetrated down the centuries. In a demonic twist, it is the ugly reason given for the crusades, the inquisitions, and the theology of hostility that darkens our world. It is ironic that the blame for such evil should be attributed to the truth of the gospel, rather than its tragic defilement and desecration. It is like blaming rape on marriage or incest on parenting. How wrong and depressing it is for Christ's followers to be embarrassed by the truth that comforts and saves.

15

Kathy has been a Christian for quite awhile and she continues to struggle with the exclusive claim of the gospel. Most of the time she quietly sets the issue aside but her concerns resurfaced recently when her discipleship group studied Acts 4:12 ("Salvation is found in no one else, for there is no other name under heaven given to mankind by which we must be saved"). On an unrelated topic, one of the women in Kathy's group shared a story about Bill, a fellow church member who attended another discipleship group. Bill's group met earlier in the week over lunch at Panera to share their one-minute personal testimonies with each other. After the meeting Bill excused himself to take a smoke outside the restaurant. With his Bible and notebook in hand, Bill was standing outside smoking a cigarette when he was approached by a young man who asked about his notebook. Bill was able to share with him what he had just shared with the group. In response, the young man shared some of his story as well. It was one full of struggle and heartache. Bill listened and then asked if he could pray for the young man, who gladly accepted. Bill looked up after praying to see a few tears running down the young man's face. He thanked Bill and went on his way.

But when Kathy heard the story she was upset. "Why would Bill have gone out to smoke?! Doesn't he realize that smoking is wrong; smoking can kill you!" Bill's joy at being able to share his faith with a stranger was overshadowed by the fact that he was a smoker. The irony here is that Kathy holds a definite conviction about smoking, but finds it difficult to hold a definite conviction about salvation. For her the truth about smoking is clear and life-threatening; but for Jesus in the upper room the truth about salvation is equally clear and eternally life-saving.

Trouble's many and diverse pathologies describe the world ("In this world you will have trouble"); truth's singularity and fidelity define salvation ("But be of good cheer for I have overcome the world"). Into our troubled and anxious world, Jesus says, "I am the way and the truth and the life." The Word made flesh reveals God *in person*, not as an abstraction or a concept or a mystical experience. "The Way, the Truth, and the Life are not three abstractions in John's Gospel; they are a single Person. This Person, Jesus, is the wonderfully focusing, simplifying, and centering revelation of God Almighty."[1]

Friendship, marriage, health, and adventure can all be described conceptually in the abstract, but until they are experienced in person, they lack their true meaning. This is how it is with God. Spirituality in the abstract may delight the imagination and challenge the intellect, but it is a weak substitute for the real encounter with the living God. Jesus is the culminating revelation of God, mediating the truth and the salvation of God to everyone personally. The appeal of the gospel is beautifully and passionately inclusive ("for God so loved the world"), because God has made himself known personally, and therefore *exclusively* ("that he gave his one and only Son that whosoever believes in him should not die but have everlasting life" [John 3:16]). The very power of the inclusivity of the gospel rests exclusively on its one and only Savior, who is the way and the truth and the life.

Our redemptive dramas capture our longing for salvation that can either be explained away by evolutionary intuition or credited to the fact that we are made in God's image and long to be safe in his Presence. One old television show caught my imagination. It was called *The Equalizer*. The lead character, Robert McCall, a former CIA agent, living in New York City, made it his calling to rescue people from violent, life-threatening situations. The victims came from all walks of life and they were always in desperate straits with no one to turn to. Enter Robert McCall. He looked the person in the eye and said, "You are not alone. I will save you." Or, "Trust me. You are safe now. I will solve this problem." And he always did! But it was in that dramatic moment of exchange between fear and trust, that McCall's confidence reminded me of Jesus looking into Thomas' eyes (looking into my eyes) and saying, "I am the way and the truth and the life."

1. Bruner, *John*, 812.

Upper Room Reflection

How can the offense of the gospel be based on the comfort of the gospel?

What is the relationship between the way and the truth and the life?

Why is it easier for us to settle for religion in the abstract than for discipleship in person?

Can others know you without knowing you in person? Can we know God apart from Jesus?

DAY 6

Is Jesus Enough?

"If you have come to know me, you will come to know my Father as well. In fact, from now on you do know him; you have even seen him.' Philip says to him: 'Lord, please show us the Father, and that will be enough for us.'"

John 14:7–8

JOHN WROTE THE FOURTH Gospel not only with Thomas and Philip in mind, but with Christ's other sheep in mind (John 10:16). The upper room disciples are a revealing picture of our own inability to embrace the truth of Jesus and to appreciate just who we have in Jesus. We read the Bible and pray. We sing hymns and listen to sermons. We do good works in Jesus' name, but like Philip, we look for more. We seem only half convinced that Jesus is enough. We want something deeper and more satisfying. We are not content with God's self-revelation.

Picture Philip face-to-face with Jesus: "Master, show us the Father; then we'll be content" (John 14:8, The Message). His well-meaning but misguided request is seemingly oblivious to the truth of the gospel: "No one has ever seen God, but the one and only Son, who is himself God and is in the closest relationship with the Father, has made him known" (John 1:18).

Since the days of Jesus, the church has had a constant struggle with Philip's underlying disappointment and the pressure to add something special to keep believers satisfied. Since we feel the need for a visible, visceral experience of the Father, we want to make up for the perceived lack in revelation with religion, ritual, and emotion. This is never said in so many words and it is never said negatively. Philip is all positive: "Lord, show us the Father and that will be enough for us." But Philip's spiritual quest for more immediate access underlies our traditional drift toward pomp and circumstance and/or our modern appetite for hype and entertainment. In lieu of simple trust in Jesus and obedience to his kingdom ethic we seem compelled to add liturgical rites or worldly strategies for church growth.

With Jesus seated at the table, in conversation with the disciples, Philip didn't realize how good they had it, and neither do we. We have grand visions of glory, inspired by magnificent cathedrals, heavenly anthems, and pulsating praise music, but the glory of Jesus, full of grace and truth, is far more personal and down to earth than we may realize. God's glory is revealed in more mundane ways than in a crowd-pleasing performance. It is evident in the unadorned altar, manna in the morning, in a Davidic psalm, and in a crown of thorns.

The golden calf "festival to the Lord" precipitated a crisis. The people of Israel wanted a visible, visceral experience of God's glory; they wanted a rock-out experience of spiritual and sensual abandonment and Aaron gave it to them. The whole episode was a disaster and when it was all over Moses went back up Mount Sinai and begged God for the promise of his Presence. "Now show me your glory," Moses said. And the Lord said, "I will cause all my goodness to pass in front of you, and I will proclaim my name, the Lord, in your presence. I will have mercy on whom I will have mercy, and I will have compassion on whom I will have compassion. But," the Lord said, "you cannot see my face, for no one may see me and live" (Exod 33:18–21). Reading God's promise to Moses in the light of Jesus' conversation with Philip, we cannot help but see Jesus as the fulfillment of the promised presence of God. All the goodness and mercy and compassion of God are revealed in his person. As Jesus said, "The one who looks at me is seeing the one who sent me" (John 12:45).

Upper Room Reflection

How have you been tempted to compensate for a perceived lack of revelation?

What are the terms of your contentment with God?

Philip knew God better than he realized. How might that be true of you as well?

How is Jesus enough for you?

DAY 7

The Invisible God Made Visible

"Jesus answered: 'Don't you know me, Philip, even after I have been among you such a long time? Anyone who has seen me has seen the Father. How can you say, 'Show us the Father?' Don't you believe that I am in the Father, and that the Father is in me? The words I say to you I do not speak on my own authority. Rather, it is the Father, living in me, who is doing his work. Believe me when I say that I am in the Father and the Father is in me; or at least believe on the evidence of the works themselves."

John 14:9–11

TWO TEACHERS APPLIED FOR the same position. One had ten years in the school system and the other five. The one with five years of teaching experience was hired. The older teacher complained to the principal, "Why wasn't I hired? I have ten years of experience, five more years than the person you hired." The principal responded somewhat undiplomatically, "No, I'm sorry. You've had only one year of experience ten times." Pastor Ray Steadman told that story years ago and it has stayed with me ever since. As I get older I have to admit it haunts me a little. Is my maturity in Christ commensurate with the years and experience I have had with the Lord Jesus? Do "I (really) press on to take hold of that for which

Christ Jesus took hold of me?" (Phil 3:12). Or, have I learned to play a religious game?

There is a sense of sadness in Jesus' response to Philip—to us, "Have I been with you all this time, Philip, and you haven't recognized me?" The question faintly recalls Yahweh's assertion on the lips of his prophets that he has made his name known (Ezek 20:9). Yahweh did everything to make himself known, yet people remained indifferent to his love. "What more could I have done for my vineyard?" (Isa 5:4). We might be tempted to post a sad spiritual axiom: the nearness of God accentuates spiritual near-sightedness. The Apostle Peter gave specific spiritual direction to keep our knowledge of our Lord Jesus Christ "from being ineffective and unproductive," so that we don't become "nearsighted and blind, forgetting that [we] have been cleansed from [our] past sins" (2 Pet 1:8–9).

The real story here, however, is not so much our failure to recognize Jesus as it is the true meaning of Jesus' real presence. "A gentle rebuke from Jesus leads to another peak point in the mountain ranges of revelation."[1] Jesus makes the invisible God visible. He asks Philip and all the rest of us, "Don't you believe that I am in the Father, and that the Father is in me?" The truth could not be stated any clearer: "Seeing Jesus the Son is seeing God the Father." Dale Bruner continues, "I do not know that we have climbed any higher in the Gospel of John than in this sentence with its claim, 'The person who has seen me has seen the Father.'" We are standing on holy ground. Bruner adds, "One feels that one should take off one's shoes at such verses."[2]

"Believe me," Jesus declares, "when I say that I am in the Father and the Father is in me." The fact that Jesus is in his very being "the invisible God, the firstborn of all creation" (Col 1:15) and "the radiance of God's glory and the exact representation of his being" (Heb 1:3) is the truth that we seek to affirm and not evade. Rudolf Bultmann, arguably one of the most famous twentieth-century

---

1. Beasley-Murray, *John*, 253.
2. Bruner, *John*, 815.

New Testament exegetes, sought to evade the essential truth of the oneness between the Father and the Son. He stripped away the meaning of the incarnation as only so much cultural myth, and salvaged an existential Jesus whose purpose was to call men and women in their moment of crisis to a self-authenticating freedom. We must read Bultmann as he wanted to be read: "All fellowship with Jesus loses its significance unless he is recognized as the one whose sole intention is to reveal God, and not to be anything for himself. . . . Jesus is nothing: he is simply and without exception the revelation of the Father."[3] For Bultmann, Jesus is exemplary of the existential self. He is not God incarnate, the redeemer, who has come to give his life a ransom for many. Bultmann argues for an existential oneness, which is radically different from the essential oneness between the Father and the Son revealed by the New Testament. He writes, "For modern man the mythological conception of the world, the conceptions of eschatology, of redeemer and of redemption, are over and done with. Is it possible to expect that we shall make a sacrifice of understanding, sacrificium intellectus, in order to accept what we cannot sincerely consider true—merely because such conceptions are suggested by the Bible?"[4]

In the tradition of the unadorned altar, the iconoclastic ark of the covenant, the Passover lamb, the genealogy of Rahab and Ruth, the Bethlehem manger, and the Roman cross, the invisible God makes himself known in person through his one and only Son. And he does this in a form no one anticipated: the God who kneels is the God who draws near and comforts us. He offers us himself, up close and personal. To Philip Jesus adds, if this isn't good enough for you, "at least believe on the evidence of the works themselves." Bruner lists them: "Water into Wine, Evangelized Samaritans, Officer's Son Healed at a Distance, Long-Sick Man Healed by a Word, Multiplied Loaves, Walking on Water, Blind

3. Bultmann, *John*, 608–9.
4. Bultmann, *Jesus Christ and Mythology*, 17.

Man's Sight, Lazarus Raising. 'What do I have to do to convince you?' one can almost hear Jesus pleading."[5]

Upper Room Reflection

Put yourself in Philip's place and describe how you would react to Jesus.

What are some of the personal evidences of God's work in your own life that are difficult to ignore or explain away?

What makes believing in God in this way compelling and attractive?

How would you describe yourself: are you more like Philip or more like Thomas?

5. Bruner, *John*, 816.

DAY 8

Greater Works

"Very truly I tell you, whoever believes in me will do the works I have been doing, and they will do even greater things than these, because I am going to the Father. And I will do whatever you ask in my name, so that the Father may be glorified in the Son. You may ask me anything in my name, and I will do it."

John 14:12–14

"VERY TRULY I TELL you" signifies something especially important, but in the light of what Jesus has just said about his essential relationship with the Father it is hard to imagine anything more important than that. Except, of course, for how this truth applies directly to us (the Holy Spirit is the next subject up and overshadows everything about this conversation). Because Jesus and the Father are one and the Son is fully vested with the Father's authority, all those who believe in Jesus will be empowered to do the works he has been doing. And then Jesus gives us something special (surprising, even shocking!) to think about, adding, "and they will do even greater things than these, because I am going to the Father." The promise of greater works sounds either mistaken or too good to be true. Who is going to top Jesus' accomplishments: "Reconcile the world to God, satisfy God's justice, reveal

God classically, exorcize the devil definitely, die carrying away the sin of the world, rise defeating death forever?"[1]

The short answer is "no one" but the long answer includes us, thankfully. The contrast between lesser and greater is not between what Jesus did and what believers can do, but between Jesus' pre-exaltation ministry and his rule and reign at the right hand of the Father. What makes these works greater is the eschatological fulfillment of the risen Lord Jesus. When the narrow and restricted limitations of the earthly ministry of Jesus are overcome in his resurrection and ascension and the outpouring of the Holy Spirit is experienced by his followers, greater works abound.

Greater in scope, because the gospel goes global. Pentecost's 3,000 new believers are added to the church many times over around the world daily. Greater in power, because now we can say with the apostle, "I can do all things through Christ who strengthens me" (Phil 4:13). Greater in comfort, because we can comfort others with the comfort that we have been comforted (2 Cor 1:4). Greater in depth, because "the Spirit intercedes for God's people in accordance with the will of God" (Rom 8:27). Greater in hope, because nothing "will be able to separate us from the love of God that is in Christ Jesus our Lord" (Rom 8:39).

I believe this "greater work" applies to the elder in our church who is a structural biologist studying ion channels and enzymatic membrane proteins. He enters his lab, the way I enter my study, with prayers that the Lord will open his mind to the truth embedded in God's revelation. This greater work extends to the vocational calling of the priesthood of all believers: nurses, doctors, plumbers, electricians, teachers, police officers, etc. If every believer is called to be a missionary, called to be a priest, called to be an evangelist, then a vast understanding of the greater things Jesus had in mind becomes real.

The greater works belong to the eschatological fulfillment of the gospel, not to our wish dreams and entrepreneurial visions. Confusion comes into play when we substitute our business

---

1. Bruner, *John*, 817.

model BHAGs (pronounced bee-hags, short for "Big Hairy Auda-
cious Goals") for the will of God. Jesus defined the greater work
in several ways: it is always in keeping with his works; it is always
dependent on him going to the Father; and it is always consistent
with his name, that is to say, his nature, character, will, and mission. When Jesus says, "You may ask me for anything in my name,
and I will do it" (John 14:14), our minds are tempted to fly off in a
million directions. If we lift the promise out of the context of Jesus'
life and ministry, if we forget the challenge to take up our cross
daily and follow Jesus, it is easy to misconstrue this bold promise
as a "blank check" for our health and wealth.

There are many things through life that I thought I wanted—
really wanted and sincerely prayed for. Like the time I applied for
a scholarship to study in England. When I became a finalist, one
of four candidates to reach the last stage, I thought for sure God
was leading my wife and me to England to further prepare for his
kingdom work. I claimed Psalm 20:4 as my verse: "May he give you
the desire of your heart and make all your plans succeed." I felt so
certain that the Lord was working this all out. My interview with
a tribunal of ten scholars and executives seemed to go very well.
They assured me that I would hear from them within forty-eight
hours. I felt so certain that the Lord was in this request that I could
have said, "I accept. Thank you. God has done this and it is marvel-
ous in our eyes!"

Well, you know where I'm headed with this, don't you? I got
my special delivery rejection notice in the mail the next day. Disappointed does not begin to describe how I felt. I was bewildered,
crushed, angry. Why did God do this to me? Why did he say, "Ask
me for anything in my name, and I will do it"? All that did was
to build up false hope, enticing me to imagine success and then
hitting me in the gut with failure. But that incident forced me
to understand God's will in a new light. I've never been quite so
certain ever since that my desires correspond perfectly with God's
will. There's plenty of room to be humble. In Psalm 20, I was driven
kicking and screaming from verse four to verse one, "May the Lord
answer you when you are in distress; may the name of the God of

Jacob protect you. May he send you help from the sanctuary and grant you support from Zion." Success in our eyes may be failure to God and failure to the world may be success to God. Jesus summed it up bluntly for the Pharisees: "What people value highly is detestable in God's sight" (Luke 16:15).

When the five missionaries gave their lives on a Curaray River sandbar in the jungle of Ecuador, January 8, 1956, no one, especially their five young wives and nine fatherless children, knew what an impact their lives would have for the kingdom of Christ. But God used "Operation Auca" in ways Jim Elliot, Pete Fleming, Ed McCully, Nate Saint, and Roger Youderian had never dreamed of. The sacrifice of their earthly lives served as a catalyst to draw worldwide attention to the Auca Indians, calling thousands to earnest prayer for the salvation of the tribe and challenging many to carry the gospel to unreached people around the world. Who can begin to measure the success of their ministries? What looked like a disaster was really a kingdom breakthrough!

Upper Room Reflection

How does Jesus carefully define the greater work?

Rightly understood, what's so great about the greater work?

When it comes to understanding God's will, have you ever had a "gut-check" experience?

"The 'whatevers' excite (sometimes, let us admit, too much); 'in my name' focuses and sobers."[2] *How have you found this observation to be true?*

---

2. Ibid., 831.

To Believe is to Obey and to Obey is to Believe

"When you love me, you will be keeping these commands of mine."

John 14:15

SOME TRANSLATIONS OF TODAY'S verse may say "if" instead of "when," but the context shows that Jesus is not questioning the disciples' love; he's assuming it. The simple future tense ("you will") instead of an imperative ("you should") implies that Jesus is anticipating their loving obedience.[1] Even though these very same disciples will cut and run, Jesus insists on the big picture and the irresistible and compelling nature of God's unbeatable grace. Denials, yes, but undying devotion and martyrdom even more so!

Loving obedience is costly. A court in Sudan sentenced a pregnant Christian Sudanese woman to death by hanging because she refused to renounce her faith in Christ. Meriam Ibrahim, twenty-seven, married a Christian man in 2011 and was eight months pregnant at the time with their second child. She was found guilty of apostasy because she converted from Islam to Christianity and of adultery because she married a Christian, a marriage not recognized by sharia law. She was sentenced to one hundred lashes for her adultery and death by hanging for her apostasy. Meriam was given three days to recant. When she faced the Moslem clerics in

1. Bruner, *John*, 835.

court, she simply said, "I am a Christian." Meriam Ibrahim's fidelity to Christ, her quiet courage, and her humble witness testify to the greater works, made possible by the resurrection and the ascension of Christ. These good works are rooted not in willpower but in God's will; not in the resilient human spirit, but in the abiding presence of Christ. Thankfully, Meriam Ibrahim's life was spared and she was released. Her faithfulness stands as a powerful testimony to her love for Christ.

Our text is a single sentence that pivots between Jesus' promise of the greater works and his gift of the Holy Spirit. The meaning of the greater works depends upon a convergence of truths: the ascension of the Son to the Father, the acceptance of the ministry and mission of the Son ("You may ask me for anything in my name"), and the faithful obedience of those who love Christ. This loving obedience flows out of a personal relationship with Jesus Christ. In the context of the upper room this single sentence makes for a good caption under the group portrait of the disciples, with all of us who follow the Lord Jesus photoshopped into the family picture.

Rudolf Bultmann made a fatal mistake. He argued that the words, "When you love me" lead to a misunderstanding. They create a false conception of an ongoing personal relationship with Jesus. Bultmann claimed that Jesus' legacy was not *himself* but his example of abandonment to the will of God. Jesus never came to establish a personal relationship with himself. Bultmann argued that the incarnation was a culture-bound myth designed to inspire self-authenticating existential freedom. He concluded that "following Jesus beyond death has been finally forgotten here."[2]

Contrary to Bultmann's ideological reading of the text, Jesus rooted our discipleship in his *atoning sacrifice* ("Unless I wash you, you have no part with me" [John 13:8]), in *our personal trust* ("You believe in God; believe also in me" [John 14:1]), in his *final coming* ("If I go and prepare a place for you, I will come back and take you to be with me that you also may be where I am" [John 14:3]), and in our *prayerful dependence* on him ("You may ask me for anything

2. Bultmann, *John*, 613.

in my name, and I will do it" [John 14:14]). The call to obedience issues out of this deep and abiding relationship with Jesus.

Marriage is a picture of love and obedience walking hand in hand. The oneness of the marriage relationship draws on the principle the cross, "my life for yours" and the principle of creation, and "the two will become one flesh." By divine design, marriage was created to point beyond itself to our union with God in Christ. The love of Christ leads a couple into the shared work of marriage. "Clothe yourselves with compassion, kindness, humility, gentleness and patience. Bear with each other and forgive whatever grievances you may have against one another. Forgive as the Lord forgave you. And over all these virtues put on love which binds them all together in perfect unity" (Col 3:12–14). The language of their vows is grandly inclusive of all they are and will be. Their comprehensive commitment is a covenant, not a contract; an enduring promise not a hope-it-works-out proposal. It is real work, but it is the kind of work they are called to do. Love in marriage works itself out in fidelity and faithfulness, mutual submission and respect, forgiveness and sacrifice, or it really isn't love at all.

When we love Jesus we will want to keep his commands, the whole range of his commands. "Loving Jesus doesn't allow me to graze at the heavenly salad bar of blessings, choosing my favorite foods and even going back for seconds but leaving the items I don't care for untouched."[3] The New Testament is very explicit on this score: "This is love for God: to keep his commands. And his commands are not burdensome, for everyone born of God overcomes the world. This is the victory that has overcome the world, even our faith. Who is it that overcomes the world? Only the one who believes that Jesus is the Son of God" (1 John 5:3–5). Pray for our sister Meriam Ibrahim, and the many sisters and brothers in Christ like her. Pray for yourself, not only that you will stand faithfully when your day comes, but that you will stand for Christ today.

---

3. Jim Eschenbrenner, personal correspondence, used with permission.

Upper Room Reflection

How can the commands of Jesus be taught and practiced as a gracious invitation rather than a legal obligation?

How have you experienced the tension between works righteousness and the work of righteousness?

How does Bultmann's misunderstanding help clarify your understanding of the text?

What helps you distinguish between cheap grace and costly grace?

DAY 10

The Spirit of Truth

"And I will ask the Father, and he will give you
another Encourager—to be with you forever—
the Spirit of the Truth."

John 14:16–17

WHEN I TRAVEL TO remote places like Mongolia or Cambodia without my wife I feel pretty far from home. I'm sensitive to the strangeness of the situation and I'm usually counting down the long days until I return home. But when my wife Virginia travels with me to some of these remote places I hardly feel that I've left home. Her friendship has a way of bringing "home" along with her to wherever we go. When she's right there with me what's the point of rushing home? That analogy gives me a tangible sense of the comfort Jesus promised when he said, "I will ask the Father, and he will give you another advocate to help you and be with you forever—the Spirit of Truth." We are not alone: even when our close friends are absent, the Lord God has our back. Along with the abiding presence of Jesus Christ (more on this later) we have another "Encourager," one who is called to come alongside (Paraclete) for the sake of the gospel. "When he comes, he will prove the world to be wrong about sin and righteousness and judgment: about sin, because people do not believe in me; about righteousness, because I am going to the Father, where you can see me no longer; and about judgment, because the prince of this world now stands condemned" (John 16:8–11).

In Greco-Roman culture *paraclete* referred to a legal adviser or advocate. If you have ever been represented by gifted lawyers, you know how crucial their knowledge and skills can be. They often work behind the scenes warning clients of unperceived dangers. They expose hidden risks and vulnerabilities. Most importantly, good lawyers honor the truth. This analogous relationship between the practice of law and the role of the Spirit may help correct the false perception some have of the Spirit as the extroverted, emotional member of the Trinity—the divine cheerleader who fires up the troops and the divine wizard who makes spectacular things happen. Based on Jesus' description, there is nothing showy or touchy-feely about the Holy Spirit.

The King James version of the Bible refers to the Spirit as the "Comforter," suggesting to today's believer personal reassurance and emotional support. But derived from its Latin root, *confortare*, comfort meant "to strengthen." The Spirit of truth strengthens the fellowship of disciples by inspiring biblical insight and faithful obedience. The Spirit helps make the previous verse possible: "When you love me, you will be keeping my commands." The Spirit encourages believers through theological understanding and ethical discernment. The fullness of the Spirit has more to do with obeying the Sermon on the Mount in practical Jesus-like ways and making disciples globally than it does with feeling a spiritual high—much more!

The Spirit is the most self-effacing member of the Trinity, even more so than the incarnate one! You might say that the Holy Spirit is the shy member of the Trinity. Good lawyers tend to do most of their work behind the scenes to save their clients from public confrontation and litigation. The best lawyers never draw attention to themselves. They have their client's back and they have their client's best interests at heart. The Holy Spirit never goes beyond Jesus and never becomes his rival. The Holy Spirit never promotes his own baptism, as if somehow baptism in the Spirit could be a second blessing and distinct from our baptism in the name of the Father, Son, and Holy Spirit. In the upper room, Jesus made it clear that it is impossible to believe in him and not have

THE GOD WHO COMFORTS

the advocacy of the Spirit. We are the passive recipients of Jesus'
active asking. Jesus asks the Father for the Spirit and the Father
gives the Spirit because Jesus asks. The Father, Son, and Holy Spirit
are locked in together, absolutely interdependent and mutually
supportive. The triune God is the best description possible for the
line "all for one and one for all." The gift of the Spirit of truth means
that we are always at home with Jesus.

Upper Room Reflection

How does the description of the Spirit as an *advocate*
influence your perception of the Spirit?

Should the oneness of the triune God impact our
understanding of the Holy Spirit?

How have you experienced the Spirit's help?

How should disciples seek for a deeper experience of the
Spirit of truth?

DAY 11

Our True Friend

"I am talking about the Spirit of Truth, whom the world cannot accept, because it does not see him or know him. Ah, but you know him, because he is making his home right here beside your fellowship now, and he will be making his home right there inside your fellowship later."

John 14:17 (Trans. by Frederick Dale Bruner)

JESUS TESTIFIES THAT THE world cannot accept the Spirit of truth, "because it does not see him or know him." His blunt assertion explains why the fellowship of believers is unacceptable to the world and why any attempt to leverage consumer appeal or to make Christianity sexy ultimately fails. We cannot appeal to the world on the world's terms without distorting the gospel. "The world *qua world* cannot receive the Spirit; to do so it would have to give up its essential nature, that makes it the world."[1] Worldly spirituality is visual and vibrant, appealing to the soul through the physical senses. The world, the flesh, and the devil can captivate the soul with a single shot on goal or an expensive acquisition. The pantheon of material gods is impressive, with each god particularized in the object of devotion (sports, success, music, fashion, adventure, etc.) and universalized like Hindu gods.

---

1. Bultmann, *John*, 616.

"Sports may be the place in contemporary life where Americans find sacred community most easily."[2] The synapses of a brain trained to the quick visual stimulus of an NFL helmet-to-helmet hit, replayed four or five times, can hardly cope with hearing the human voice preach the Word of God. The sensual atmosphere of heart-throbbing international soccer is hardly on a level playing field with singing worship songs. True worship is bound to be a challenge for sports junkies hooked on the game's adrenaline rush. Can we watch the second-to-second high-impact visual impressions of the NBA or the NFL or MLB and learn to pray the Psalms? Within the inner sanctum of today's home entertainment centers, Christians are mentally, emotionally, and physically manipulated and captivated by the game. No wonder Christians are bored when they come to church. Tertullian, an early church leader, asked "What does Jerusalem have to do with Athens?" We might ask, what does Sunday morning worship have to do with a fifty-five inch Sony Hi-Definition flat-screen tuned to ESPN?

Oprah Winfrey is a "a post-modern priestess—an icon of church-free spirituality."[3] Her life is "a window into American spirituality" that rivals the gospel of Jesus Christ. Oprah's glossy magazine promotes a secular religion that is based on covenant between Oprah and her readers: "She will keep exhorting you to improve, and you will keep trying. . . . Her fans apparently want to be told that great truths can be found in shallow books; that it's all right to hate men, or not; to ditch your marriage, or save it; to lose weight, or wear it proudly; to conceal your age, or accept it; to have a sex change, or change back; to abandon your child, or raise your child; to cherish your family, or relish your singleness. . . . She has achieved a kind of perfection, slinging truths, half-truths, and outright nonsense to flatter America with its own favorite fallacies."[4] Her "gospel of empowerment" gives women hope that they can improve themselves and change their life situ-

2. Dreyfus and Kelly, *All Things Shining*, 192.
3. Taylor, "The Church of Oprah Winfrey," 40.
4. Skinner, "In Oprah We Trust," 22, 26.

ation through an eclectic spirituality that encourages them to take what they like and leave what they don't like. "One of the biggest mistakes humans make," Oprah says, "is to believe there is only one way. Actually, there are many diverse paths leading to what you call God."[5]

The pressure is on in today's "show me the money" culture to make something impressive of Christianity, to put something attractive and compelling alongside the gospel to make it more appealing, to visualize Christianity in liturgical aesthetics or trendy worship or charismatic personalities. But this temptation violates the ancient prohibition against showy altars and self-serving performances. God concluded the Ten Commandments with specific instructions on how not to worship him. "Do not make any gods to be alongside me; do not make for yourselves gods of silver or gods of gold" (Exod 20:23). The temptation today is over what comes alongside the fellowship of disciples, the Paraclete or a market strategy; the Paraclete or a charismatic motivational speaker; the Paraclete or self-help strategies; the Paraclete or liturgical formality. All of our worldly effort only gets in the way of the promised Holy Spirit, the Paraclete, who comes *alongside* the fellowship of disciples "to create a Christ-centered Church."[6]

Herein lies the challenging, yet comforting truth of Jesus' blunt spiritual direction: friendship with the Spirit of truth means enmity with the world. It is comforting because it is clarifying. We don't need to be in doubt about the world's reaction to Christ and the gospel. In his letter, John writes, "Do not love the world or anything in the world. If anyone loves the world, love for the Father is not in them. For everything in the world—the lust of the flesh, the lust of the eyes, and the pride of life—comes not from the Father but from the world. The world and its desires pass away, but whoever does the will of God lives forever" (1 John 2:15–17). We have chosen a friend, or even better the friend has chosen us, and that friendship means more to us than the world's acceptance.

5. Taylor, "The Church of Oprah Winfrey," 45.
6. Bruner, *John*, 835.

Furthermore, if we are going to be any help to the world we want to hold close to this friend. The Holy Spirit, Jesus' authorized personal representative, is our best advocate in the world.

When Duane Litfin was president of Wheaton College he was asked to offer the invocation at a secular academic gathering. Since he is a Christian and believes that "there is one mediator between God and human beings, the man Christ Jesus" (1 Tim 2:5), he prays in the name of Jesus. Aware of the current social climate and the power of Jesus' name to divide, he did not want to put the convener in jeopardy. So he asked him, "Do you think it will be a problem in this gathering for me to pray in Jesus' name?" The convener thought for a moment and then replied that, yes, he thought that would be a problem. Litfin acknowledges that God has nowhere ordained that he must explicitly use those exact words, and in fact he does not always conclude his prayers that way. Yet here was a case where he was being asked to distance himself from Jesus for the sake of the sensibilities of others, and to acquiesce in that unspoken premise of American civil religion that stipulates that all ways to God are equally valid.[7]

Litfin explains that he settled this dilemma in his own mind long ago. Suppose the convener had said to him, "Look, we want you to come to this meeting, but please do not bring your wife. Some at this gathering find her offensive. We're happy to have you, but please don't mention her name." What would he have done then? In the same way, this situation was requiring that he disassociate himself from the name of Jesus. He was being forced to choose, which meant that he had no choice at all, precisely because, as in his marriage, that choice was made long ago. Jesus said, "Whoever is ashamed of me and my words in this adulterous and sinful generation, of him will the Son of man also be ashamed when he comes in the glory of his Father with the holy angels" (Mark 8:38).

Jesus reassures the disciples that they already know the Spirit, "for he lives with you and will be in you." Spirituality is a personal experience of the abiding presence of the Holy Spirit in the

7. Litfin, *Conceiving the Christian College*, 82.

fellowship of believers. We are at home with the three-personed God. To know Jesus is to know the Father (14:9) and the Spirit (14:17) in community.

Upper Room Reflection

How do you react to being told that the Spirit of truth is rejected by the world?

Which of the world's rival spiritualities has the biggest impact on people?

Why does the Spirit of truth draw opposition?

Would you have responded the way Duane Litfin did?

DAY 12

You Are Not Alone

"I will not leave you as orphans; I will come to you.
Before long, the world will not see me anymore, but you
will see me. Because I live, you also will live."

John 14:18–19

THE PROMISE OF JESUS' coming defines the deep meaning of his comfort. Four distinct comings shape Jesus' discipleship sermon in the upper room: his final coming, the Parousia; his gift of the Spirit, the Paraclete; his death and resurrection, the Passion; and his abiding fellowship, the Presence. These four comings are the ways in which Jesus draws near. They are meant to shape the relational expectations of Christ's followers, giving our lives meaning and purpose, all because we belong to Christ. Jesus reassures his followers that they are not alone. Sin separates us from God, from his creation, from one another, and from ourselves, but in Christ we are reconciled, reborn, reunited, and renewed. Between the upper room and heaven, the God who comforts does everything he can to make us feel at home until we *finally* get home.

The promise of the Spirit is experienced most personally not in private, but in and through the fellowship of believers. The Southern dialect draws out the second person plural: "But *y'all* know him, for he lives with *y'all* and will be in *y'all*." We don't look for the Spirit in the interior recesses of ourselves, as much as in the company of our brothers and sisters in Christ. This is why devoting ourselves to the Word of God, to close fellowship and practical sharing, to Eucharistic worship, and to prayer are so vital to the experience of the Spirit (Acts 2:42). The coming of the Spirit, as requested by the Son and sent by the Father, is predicated on the risen Lord Jesus. It is for that reason that Jesus turns our attention to his resurrection.

Although Gethsemane and a long night of trials awaited him, Jesus persisted in being the encourager. "I will not leave you as orphans: I will come to you." Initially the disciples saw the cross as a tragic failure. From their perspective Jesus' mission came to a disastrous end, leaving the disciples in the lurch. Three years of flat-out commitment and inspiring expectations were dead-ending in a religious conspiracy and a political cross. Over the course of the night this despair gripped the imagination of the disciples. But in the upper room Jesus overcame the defeatist scenario with his own narrative. His bold promise is a straightforward indicative. He speaks with simplicity and certainty. He sows the seed of hope in the soil of their confusion and despair. When the disciples look back and relive the conversation they will remember the earnestness and determination of his encouragement.

The promise, "I will not leave you as orphans" (deprived of parents) sounds like something one would say to children, not Galilean fishermen. When young parents go away on a trip they never say to their children, "I will not leave you as orphans," but they think about it. What parent isn't nervous about some unforeseen disaster leaving their young children orphaned? When our children were young we named a couple in our will who agreed to parent our children if we died. We did not want to leave them parentless—orphans.

The language Jesus used is deeply personal. He underscored his intimate bond with his disciples. It is on the order of parent and child, recalling the promise in the prologue: "Yet to all who did receive him, to those who believed in his name, he gave the right to become children of God—children born not of natural descent, nor of human decision or a husband's will, but born of God" (John 1:12–13).

The world will use the cross to put an end to Jesus, and to that ugly fact Jesus simply says, "Before long the world will not see me anymore." The world remains the world, entrenched in rebellion and disbelief, as oblivious and resistant to the resurrection as it was to Jesus' incarnation and teaching. At the cross Jesus concludes his in-person revelations to the world. There will be no resurrection appearances to the world, even though we might imagine like Judas (not Iscariot) the extraordinary impact of such a revelation (John 14:22). But to the disciples, Jesus promised, "You will see me. Because I live, you also will live." Jesus reserved his resurrection appearances between Easter and the ascension for his disciples, and the impact of their testimony changed the course of history. The meaningfulness of Jesus' bodily resurrection can be explored from many angles, but the one emphasized by Jesus in the upper room is the extraordinary relational comfort of his real resurrection. "Because I live, you also will live." This is the comfort with which we have been comforted (1 John 1:1–4).

In the midst of his hellish suffering, Job fought his way to the conclusion that human existence was more than chance and fate, and a few short years of pleasure and pain. He wanted the truth of God and his own destiny engraved on his soul. Although he was crushed he clung to one enduring hope. "Oh, that my words were recorded, that they were written on a scroll, that they were inscribed with an iron tool on lead, or engraved in rock forever! I know that my Redeemer lives, and that in the end he will stand on earth. And after my skin has been destroyed, yet in my flesh I will see God; I myself will see him with my own eyes—I, and not another. How my heart yearns within me!" (Job 19:23–27).

This is not merely a devotional truth. Job's message is essential truth for philosophy, history, biology, and theology. Sooner or later we all suffer, and when we do, we have to choose between nature alone or the God who created nature—the God who is independent of nature. We have to choose between Jesus and Nietzsche, or Jesus and Oprah, or Jesus and Dawkins. The choice is not between faith and science, but between the majesty of God and the futility of human existence apart from God.

We have a huge decision to make: are we the holy possession of God in Christ, personally chosen by God, predestined for communion with God, adopted into the community of God's people, recipients of God's grace, redeemed by his personal sacrifice on our behalf, and signed, sealed, and delivered by the promised Holy Spirit, *or* are we cosmic orphans, the accidental product of an impersonal universe, subject to blind chance and random forces, existing in a sphere of energy devoid of promise, plan, purpose, and fulfillment?

Upper Room Reflection

How can we apply Jesus' encouragement to our times of loneliness?

Where is the best place to look for the comforting presence of Christ?

What can we learn from Jesus' consistent message of comfort in the face of trials?

How has the promise of eternal life impacted your daily life?

DAY 13

The Holy Family

*"At that moment you will know absolutely that I'm in
my Father, and you're in me, and I'm in you."*

John 14:20, THE MESSAGE

MY WIFE AND I live in a front-porch community, with sidewalks, street lamps, and flower beds. Garages are off back alleys. The design encourages people to know their neighbors. The layout of our neighborhood reminds me of the relational theology revealed in the Bible. In a manner of speaking, the three-personed God is the front-porch, relational God. The underlying truth of Jesus' reassurance goes back to Genesis and the simple sentence, "Let us make human beings in our image, in our likeness" (Gen 1:26). The pronoun "us" is both subtle and startling. Humanity made in the image of God is mystery enough but the interpersonal character of God awakens an even deeper mystery. To be made in the image of God means more than a list of attributes. It is to be brought into a dynamic interpersonal relationship. We are not the product of a solitary God, but the personal creation of the living God who is social through and through. God chose to image the divine self, not in stars and beasts, but in human beings—male and female. At the core of our human identity is a capacity to relate to God and to one another like no other creature in creation, and this capacity is based on the being of God who is already a communion of persons.

The initial phrase, "Then God said," is singular, but the verb "Let us make" is plural. The intentional paradox between

46

singularity and plurality confirms the subtle distinction in Genesis 1:1–2 between God and the Spirit of God. When human creation is described, our attention is diverted from ourselves and drawn back to the mystery of God by the simple words "us" and "our." It is as if we were listening to an artist describe a particular work that all the art critics praised as his masterpiece. Our attention is drawn to the work of art as he describes how he painted it, but when he unexpectedly shifts to why he painted it our eyes instinctively focus on the artist.

In the upper room all eyes are on Jesus when he says, "On that day you disciples will know for sure that I am locked into my Father and that you are locked into me, and that I am locked into you" (14:20).[1] Jesus confirms that the disciples' personal eyewitness experience of his bodily resurrection is the key to their new self-understanding. And not only their self-understanding but ours as well. "All future disciples of Jesus may legitimately transfer this remark of Jesus to their own lives, for they are in a chain of disciples who are in fellowship with history's single most significant person and event."[2] The apostles were sensitive to the fact that future believers were dependent on their witness and the Holy Spirit's confirmation. They held this responsibility in the highest regard. John wrote, "The life appeared; we have seen it and testify to it, and we proclaim to you the eternal life, which was with the Father and has appeared to us. We proclaim to you what we have seen and heard, so that you also may have fellowship with us. And our fellowship is with the Father and with his Son, Jesus Christ" (1 John 1:2–3). Peter praised God for giving us "new birth into a living hope through the resurrection of Jesus Christ from the dead. . . . Though you have not seen him, you love him; and even though you do not see him now, you believe in him and are filled with an inexpressible and glorious joy, for you are receiving the end result of your faith, the salvation of your souls" (1 Peter 1:3, 8–9). The disciples remembered what Jesus said to Thomas, "Because you

1. Bruner, *John*, 839.
2. Ibid., 840.

have seen me, you have believed; blessed are those who have not seen and yet have believed" (John 20:29).

If we are inclined to envy the upper room disciples for their sensory experience of the risen Christ ("that . . . which we have heard, which we have seen with our eyes, which we have looked at and our hands have touched . . ." [1 John 1:1]), we should remember that we will one day see him as he is. "For now we see only a reflection as in a mirror; then we shall see face to face. Now I know in part; then I shall know fully, even as I am fully known" (1 Cor 13:12).

Faith does not operate in a different realm from sight. Faith is the earnest expectation of sight. In the most real world the two are inseparably linked and inherent in objective reality. "Without faith," wrote the author of Hebrews, "it is impossible to please him, for whoever would draw near to God must believe that he exists and that he rewards those who earnestly seek him" (Hebrews 11:6). Sight does not create that which is seen, nor does faith create that which is believed. If seeing meant believing for the first disciples, then believing means seeing for today's disciples. The resurrection of Christ is a fact of science and history that is believed by faith. If the resurrection of Christ did not actually happen in real time and real history, the Apostle Paul spelled out the verdict: our faith is useless and we are guilty of bearing false witness. We are still in our sins and we are lost, without hope in the world. "If in this life only we have hoped in Christ, we are of all people most to be pitied" (1 Cor 15:19).

Upper Room Reflection

What does it mean to you to be "locked into" God the Father, Son, and Holy Spirit?

How does Jesus' promised communion with God counter our bent toward individualism?

How would you describe the moment of realization when you knew Jesus to be the risen Lord? How do you think about the relationship between faith and sight?

DAY 14

Real Love

"Whoever has my commands and keeps them is the one who loves me. The one who loves me will be loved by my Father, and I too will love them and show myself to them."

John 14:21

THE BEST SPIRITUAL DIRECTION often comes in conversation, not in preaching or lecturing. We may be drawn to a logical presentation of well-ordered, well-argued points, but a good conversation often encourages the dynamic interplay between the personal and the conceptual. Conversations, like the one in the upper room, blend invitation and engagement in a lively dialogue. The setting is intimate. Face-to-face communication fosters the exchange between the eleven disciples and Jesus. Questions can be asked, body language read, understanding sealed with a nod. Jesus humbly hosted the meal. He made the arrangements and washed the disciples' feet. On his knees he taught the deep truth of the atonement and the practical meaning of discipleship. He addressed the painful subjects of betrayal and denial. His humility amplified their hearing and their hearing amplified his truth. Jesus' discipleship sermon is an endearing farewell and an inspiring manifesto. His spiraling intensity of comfort and challenge propels the conversation forward into our hearts and minds.

Jesus returns repeatedly to the importance of loving obedience. It is the like the refrain of a hymn sung after each stanza.

Woven into the meaning of the atonement and the praxis of discipleship and the goings and comings of Jesus is the theme, "If you love me, keep my commands." News of his imminent departure leads him to say, "A new command I give you: Love one another. As I have loved you, so you must love one another. By this everyone will know that you are my disciples, if you love one another" (John 13:34).

His oneness with the Father and his request for the Spirit of truth on our behalf frames the next reminder: "Very truly I tell you, whoever believes in me will do the works I have been doing, and they will do even greater things than these, because I am going to the Father" (John 15:12). "If you love me, keep my commands" (John 15:15).

Jesus repeats the theme of loving obedience again following his promised resurrection appearance and the disciples' understanding of his oneness with the Father: "Whoever has my commands and keeps them is the one who loves me" (John 15:21). Then again, following the other Judas's question, Jesus says, "Anyone who loves me will obey my teaching. My Father will love them, and we will come to them and make our home with them. Anyone who does not love me will not obey my teaching" (John 15:23–24).

Jesus' emphasis on loving obedience continues with the metaphor of the vine and the branches: "If you keep my commands, you will remain in my love, just as I have kept my Father's commands and remain in his love" (John 15:10).

Jesus' repeated emphasis on love made real in obedience may surprise some believers who believe that the emphasis should be more on grace than works. Doctrinaire Christians have a habit of pitting works righteousness against the work of righteousness. They misunderstand the meaning of grace. They think that since Christ paid it all nothing much is expected of them. Life goes along merrily with all of its worldly distractions and pursuits until death happens or Christ comes again. Grace is their spiritual life insurance policy. From Sunday to Sunday preachers assuage the guilty consciences of their worldly believers by quoting Romans as their signature benediction, "There is now no condemnation for those who are in Christ Jesus" (Rom 8:1). They send believers into the world armed with grace as an excuse to pursue their selfish dreams without the dire warning that "if your right eye causes you to stumble, gouge it out and throw it away" or the clear prohibition, "You cannot serve both God and Money" (Matt 5:29; 6:24).

Dietrich Bonhoeffer exposed this mentality as the deadly enemy of the church. He called it cheap grace: "Cheap grace is grace without discipleship, grace without the cross, grace without Jesus Christ, living and incarnate."[1] Bonhoeffer insisted that the New Testament marries the call to obedience and the gift of grace. To believe is to obey and to obey is to believe. Belief without obedience is cheap grace and obedience without belief is works righteousness.[2]

"Grace is costly," wrote Bonhoeffer, "because it calls us to follow, and it is grace because it calls us to follow Jesus Christ. It is costly because it costs a person his life, and it is grace because it gives a person the only true life. It is costly because it condemns sin, and grace because it justifies the sinner. Above all, it is costly because it cost God the life of his Son: 'you were bought at a price,' and what has cost God much cannot be cheap for us. Above all, it is grace because God did not reckon his Son too dear a price to pay for our life, but delivered him up for us. Costly grace is the Incarnation of God."[3] "Costly grace and sacrificial obedience are woven into the tapestry of God's love for us. One cannot be separated from the other without destroying the whole tapestry."[4]

1. Bonhoeffer, *The Cost of Discipleship*, 47.
2. Ibid., 69, 74.
3. Ibid., 47–48.
4. Jim Eschenbrenner, personal correspondence, used with permission.

Upper Room Reflection

How does the extended conversation in the upper room appeal to your understanding?

Are you surprised by Jesus' emphasis on obedience?

Is it possible to command love?

How would you describe the difference between cheap grace and costly grace?

53

DAY 15

New Commandment Evangelism

"Then Judas (not Judas Iscariot) said, 'But, Lord, why do you intend to show yourself to us and not to the world?' Jesus replied, "Anyone who loves me will obey my teaching. My Father will love them, and we will come to them and make our home with them. Anyone who does not love me will not obey my teaching. These words you hear are not my own; they belong to the Father who sent me."

John 14:22–24

UNLIKE THOMAS'S SKEPTICAL QUESTION ("Lord, we don't know where you are going . . .") or Philip's clueless question ("Lord, show us the Father and that will be enough for us"), Judas's question makes good sense: "But, Lord, why do you intend to show yourself to us and not to the world?"[1] Surely an appearance from Jesus, let's say from the pinnacle of the temple, would go a long way in convincing the world to vote for King Jesus. As far as the disciples were concerned, up until now, the movement ran on Jesus' public appearances. His crowd-gathering presence, his healing miracles, his authoritative teaching, and his confrontations with the religious leaders were all part of the daily experience of following Jesus. It would be difficult for the disciples to imagine the movement continuing if Jesus walked off the world stage.

---

1. Judas may be Judas son of James as in Luke 6:16 and Acts 1:13.

Jesus' answer is indirect, almost oblique, designed it seems to create an unexpected reaction from the disciples. Judas likely envisioned a political kingdom, a nationalistic breakthrough and takeover in fulfillment of Zionist prophecies and aspirations. But Jesus refused to go there on purpose. Why try to revamp the disciples' false expectations, when in a matter of hours the cross will smash their nationalistic hopes once and for all? Instead, he emphasized the only leverage possible for convincing the world of the gospel—obedience. "Anyone who loves me will obey my teaching."

This puts obedience in a whole new light. Jesus' kingdom ethic is essential for drawing people to Christ. The Sermon on the Mount is a practical description of the believer's real world impact. Obedience is the key. Jesus' promise of the easy yoke, "Take my yoke upon you and learn from me" (Matt 11:29), finds its fulfillment in the Sermon. The meaning of the great commandment, "Love the Lord your God with all you heart and with all your soul and with all your mind . . . and your neighbor as yourself" (Matt 22:37), is illustrated in the Sermon on the Mount. The challenge of the great commission, "Go and make disciples of all nations, baptizing them in the name of the Father and of the Son and of the Holy Spirit, teaching them to obey everything I have commanded you" (Matt 28:19–20), is worked out in the Sermon on the Mount. These summations of the gospel of grace make the Sermon on the Mount absolutely necessary. Here is the teaching we need for the abundant life (John 10:10) and for presenting our bodies as living sacrifices (Rom 12:1–2). It is the sum and substance of the Jesus way.

Eight beatitudes coupled with two affirmations, *you are* the salt of the earth and *you are* the light of the world, add up to a tenfold description of the believer. Nothing has been earned or merited by our goodness. Everything is by grace in lieu of our sin and need. Matthew and Paul agree on this: "For it is by grace you have been saved, through faith—and this not from yourselves, it is the gift of God, not by works, so that no one can boast" (Eph 2:8–9). Seven commands follow in the Sermon, just as good works follow for those created in Christ Jesus (Eph 2:10). The first command is to take the Word of God seriously. Jesus did not come to destroy but to fulfill the Law and the Prophets. "Jesus tells us how he feels about God's law before he delivers his exposition of that law at six salient points. A command to take God's law seriously is a command, too."[2]

Jesus' description of beatitude-based obedience, the kind that surpasses the righteousness of the scribes and Pharisees, focuses on our relationship to others. All six commands relate to people. Anger, lust, and divorce all deal with close relationships while oaths, revenge, and hate have more to do with social relations. Religion used the law to set limits on human aggression; Jesus used the law to show the full extent of love. The law was first given to define and deal with the reality of sin and evil. The law was given by Jesus to define and reveal the gospel of reconciliation. The difference between the Pharisees and Jesus was the difference between laying down the law for a group of prison inmates and living out the law of love in a family. In prison, the goal is to keep inmates from hurting one another. In a family the goal is to show love to one another.

For each of these seven commands, Jesus set up an antithesis between the old way of understanding the command and the new way of obeying the command. He came not to explain away the Word of God but to fulfill it. Jesus expected the Sermon on the Mount to be applied personally and practically. In the remaining six commands he illustrated how this was to be done. Jesus called for "unusual Christians in all the usual situations."[3] True obedience means love instead of hate, purity instead of lust, and fidelity instead of infidelity, honesty instead of duplicity, reconciliation instead of retaliation, and prayer instead of revenge.

Obedience is not only the key to the evangelistic appeal of the gospel but it is also essential for true spirituality. People can tell when the triune God, Father, Son, and Holy Spirit, comes to us and becomes our one true home. The evidence for knowing God and being known by God is found in obedience. It is not the truth

2. Bruner, *The Churchbook: Matthew*, vol. 1, 196.

3. Ibid., 206.

we know that counts, but the truth we live. Evangelism is primarily about living, not talking. Spirituality is primarily about obeying, not feelings. The God who comforts has gone home to the Father to prepare a dwelling place for us, but in the meantime God indwells the believer through the Spirit (John 14:26) and the abiding presence of Christ (John 15:4).

The relational evidence cuts both ways. "Anyone who does not love me will not obey my teaching" (John 14:24). This is a sober reminder that we cannot separate Jesus from his word. If we refuse to take his commands seriously, we refuse him, and not only him, but the Father. "These words you hear are not my own; they belong to the Father who sent me" (John 14:24). The relationship between the Father and the Son is tight, locked in. The disobedient cannot claim "God's love" trumps the teachings of Jesus. Jesus concluded the Sermon on the Mount on a similar theme. "Not everyone who says to me, 'Lord, Lord,' will enter the kingdom of heaven, but only the one who does the will of my Father who is in heaven" (Matt 7:21).

Upper Room Reflection

If you were Judas how would you have responded to Jesus' unexpected answer?

Does Jesus' emphasis on obedience surprise you?

How should believers determine the practical specifics of this obedience?

How does spiritual formation and ethical practice cover the same ground?

DAY 16

Everything

"I have said these things to you while I am still here at home with you. But the True Friend, the Holy Spirit, whom the Father will send in my name, that Spirit will teach you everything [you ever need to know], and he will [do that] by reminding you of everything I ever said to you."

John 14:25–26 (Trans. by Frederick Dale Bruner)

INNOVATION IS CRITICAL TO business success. Research and discovery are fundamental to scientific breakthroughs. But *remembering* is essential for discipleship. The truth we need to know has already been given to us. All our "Christian" talk of cutting-edge ministries, vision casting, rebranding, and promoting relevancy are beside the point. The investment of time and energy in the hotly touted next big thing only distracts disciples from the real work of obedience. Instead of living in the truth we already know we get sidetracked by trendy gimmicks and techniques. "Everything we need to know for Church renewal and for world mission is already present in some fresh, relevant way in faithful evangelical (gospel) exposition."[1] The Apostle Peter said it this way: "Grace and peace be yours in abundance through the knowledge of God and of Jesus our Lord. His divine power has given us everything we need for a

---

1. Bruner, *John*, 846.

godly life through our knowledge of him who called us by his own glory and goodness" (2 Pet 1:2–3).

Our shared mission is to remember, remind, and refresh, rather than innovate, invent, and reimagine. It is not our place to renegotiate the meaning of God's revelation to make it more culturally adaptable and appealing. Our responsibility is to consistently, creatively, and faithfully remember everything the Spirit teaches and everything Jesus ever said. The Apostle Peter pledged himself to this calling. He wrote, "So I will always remind you of these things, even though you know them and are firmly established in the truth you now have. I think it is right to refresh your memory as long as I live . . ." (2 Pet 1:12–13).

After the resurrection, John referred explicitly to the disciples remembering the significance of Jesus' temple-cleansing actions in the light of Old Testament prophecy (John 2:17; Ps 69:9). And after Jesus entered Jerusalem on Palm Sunday, John recalls, "Only after Jesus was glorified did they realize that these things had been written about him and that these things had been done to him" (John 12:16). "These two occasions of 'remembering' in the time following Easter and the coming of the Spirit provide illustrations of what is meant by the Spirit 'reminding' the disciples of what Jesus said: he not only enables them to recall these things but to perceive their significance, and so he teaches the disciples to grasp the revelation of God brought by Jesus in its richness and profundity."[2]

Jesus' promise of the Spirit is not limited to the first band of disciples. The Spirit of truth not only taught the first generation of believers but continues to teach every generation of believers. The New Testament is the product of the Spirit's teaching, but the Spirit's inspiration is not limited to the text alone but extends to the illuminating expositions of the Word of God through the centuries and today.

Everything that the Spirit teaches is everything that Jesus taught. Everything. On behalf of the risen Christ, the Spirit opens up the whole counsel of God to its fulfillment in Christ. Instead of

2. Beasley-Murray, *John*, 261.

"dumbing down" the gospel story and editing the canon for what we find relevant, we need a fresh grasp of the whole counsel of God. There is an unnecessary mystique that surrounds the Bible that keeps even earnest believers from grasping its meaning. We make the text out to be unwieldy and complicated. We have parsed, translated, exegeted, researched, debated, and interpreted the text, to the point of abstraction and learned sophistry. Paradoxically, in our sermonizing we have reduced the Bible to sound bites, Power-Point outlines and anecdotal illustrations.

Many churchgoing readers see the Bible as a huge undifferentiated mass of spiritual material designed to inspire devotional daily thoughts. Or, they see it as the good book with secrets for success and stories of courage. For others, the Bible has the same aura as the Islamic Koran or the Hindus Vedas—a strange religious document best interpreted by experts.

In the Spirit we grasp the finite text and proclaim its infinite meaning. Beautiful music relies on twelve pitches. The artist works with a palate of five primary colors. The periodic table is made of ninety-two natural elements. The English language has twenty-six letters. The Bible is knowable: its literary forms are recognizable; its history is manageable; and its revelation of God is comprehensible. Open up your Bible to the table of contents and you see sixty-six books listed in order of their purpose and genre. The first five books are commonly known as The Books of Moses and are foundational to the rest of the Bible. They tell the story of God's creation of the world, from the cosmos to the first human couple and from the nations to the covenant people of Israel. God conceives, redeems, identifies, and gathers a people for himself to be a blessing to the nations. Twelve history books follow, from Joshua to Esther, charting the course of this tiny beleaguered people through Israel's early history. Then, the Wisdom Books explore the human experience in relationship to God and each other: Job, Psalms, Proverbs, Ecclesiastes, and Song of Songs. The rest of the Old Testament is made up of prophets, sixteen of them from Isaiah to Malachi. The prophets are confrontational. Their job is to declare the judgment of God against all sin and rebellion and the salvation of God for all those who turn to God in humility, repentance, and faith. The tension in the text is between judgment and salvation—between the fallen condition focus and God's redemptive provision.

The New Testament consists of five stories, twenty-one letters, and one visionary poem. The Four Gospels place Jesus in the context of all that has gone before. He is the culmination and climax of all the Law and the Prophets. Everything points to him. They tell the story of Jesus in the street language of the day. Matthew, Mark, Luke, and John use the Jesus way to communicate his personal encounters, parables, miracles, and messages. They take us to the cross and the empty tomb. Acts tells us the story of Christ and the early church. Luke picks up the narrative of the risen Lord Jesus and describes how the church grew from Jerusalem to Rome. The twenty-one letters give apostolic shape to the emerging mission of God. All their theology is practical. Nothing is esoteric and abstract. Everything involves the day-to-day life of the church on the move. Sin and salvation, worship and judgment, mission and love get worked out in the real world. No one is playing church or going through the motions. John's Revelation brings the canon to an end. In the Spirit, he orchestrates a powerful symphony of countervailing tensions, worship and judgment, judgment and worship.

The whole Word of God ties together beautifully. Yet this convergence of meaning cannot be reduced to paint-by-number simplicity or PowerPoint bullets. There is nothing clever or ingenious or contrived about this weaving together of biblical truth. The entrepreneur innovates. The scientist discovers. But the disciple remembers. Fresh insights and challenging applications, yes, but everything that needs to be said has been said. The secrets of the kingdom of God have been given to us. Let's listen up!

Upper Room Reflection

Is our greatest challenge understanding the Word of God or understanding our culture?

Does the absence of new revelations make the old revelations boring?

How can you share in Peter's ministry of remembering?

What can you do to have a better grasp of the whole counsel of God?

DAY 17

Shalom

"Peace I leave with you; my peace I give you. I do not give to you as the world gives. Do not let your hearts be troubled and do not be afraid."

John 14:27

SHALOM ON THE LIPS of Jesus is more than a salutation, it is salvation. Jesus transforms a simple one-word greeting or fare-well—*peace*—into a summary of all the comfort and blessing he promised. "My peace I give you." This is the peace of Christ's aton-ing sacrifice and the peace of his new commandment love. This is the peace of the final Parousia and the gift of the Paraclete. This is the peace of the loving Father and the peace that empowers our loving obedience. "Peace I leave with you; my peace I give you" is the theme that runs through Jesus' upper room discipleship sermon. On an evening of betrayal and denial and on a clearly foreseen long night of agony, injustice, and beatings, Jesus repeats, "Do not let your hearts be troubled . . ." (John 14:1, 27).

Loving obedience begins with a seemingly impossible com-mand. How can we "let the peace of Christ rule in our hearts" (Col 3:15) when all hell breaks loose and our world comes crashing down? Humanly speaking peace of heart is easily conquered by circumstances and situations beyond our control. Relying on our own strength we readily transpose Jesus' command into pious pro-paganda, repeating the mantra, "peace, peace," into our troubled souls, when there is no peace.

✶
 We cannot create shalom, any more than we can save ourselves. We are poor candidates for peace. Our bodies break down.
People fail us. Terrorists attack. Friends betray us and war breaks
out. The world's strategies for obtaining peace have proven su-
perficial and unsuccessful. The prophet Jeremiah condemned the
religious people of his day and the complicity of their leaders.
They condoned sin instead of condemning sin. "They dress the
wound of my people as though it were not serious." They gave false
comfort, saying "Peace, peace," but there was no peace (Jer 6:14).
Their watchword was "shalom" but they defined peace "merely as
the absence of turmoil and social conflict, and not as the triumph
of divine righteousness among people."[1]

Jesus distinguished the true gift of peace from worldly peace:
"My peace I give you. I do not give to you as the world gives."
When Jesus made this distinction the Pax Romana was the iconic
standard for worldly peace, a peace achieved through superpower
military strength and political domination. The *Ara Pacis* (Latin
for "Altar of Peace") was dedicated by the Roman Senate in Rome,
in 9 BC, to celebrate Caesar and the Imperial Cult. Located on the
northern outskirts of Rome on the flood plain of the Tiber River,
the altar was a shrine to Roman civil religion. The marble walls sur-
rounding the altar depict finely sculpted scenes of life-sized men,
women, and children paying homage to the gods and goddesses.
The *Ara Pacis* symbolized Rome's pluralistic ideology of peace:
the blessings of cosmic fate, military might, and abundant fertil-
ity. Rome's eventual demise led to the neglect of the shrine. Over
the centuries it became buried under silt from the Tiber River. It
was rediscovered in the sixteenth century and excavated in 1937
in honor of the 2,000th anniversary of Caesar Augustus's birth.
Benito Mussolini rededicated it in 1938 to glorify Fascist Italy.

Simeon foresaw the price of peace when he held the baby
Jesus in his arms and said to Mary, "This child is destined to
cause the falling and rising of many in Israel, and to be a sign that
will be spoken against, so that the thoughts of many hearts will

---

1. Harrison, *Jeremiah & Lamentations*, 123.

be revealed. And a sword will pierce your own soul too" (Luke 2:34–35). Jesus knew that the gift of peace would be scorned by many. This is why he said, "Do not suppose that I have come to bring peace to the earth. I did not come to bring peace, but a sword" (Matt 10:34). This prompted Oswald Chambers to write, "Jesus Christ came to 'bring . . . a sword' through every kind of peace that is not based on a personal relationship with Himself."[2] And John Calvin said, "Peace with God is contrasted with every form of intoxicated security in the flesh."[3] Jesus was under no illusion that the world would find his peace acceptable. His followers can expect to experience trials and tribulation in the world, but ultimately the peace of Christ will prevail. "I have told you these things," Jesus said, "so that in me you may have peace. In this world you will have trouble. But take heart! I have overcome the world" (John 16:33).

The God of comfort is the Prince of Peace (Isa 9:6). "Surely he took up our infirmities and carried our sorrows, yet we considered him stricken by God, smitten by him, and afflicted. But he was pierced for our transgressions, he was crushed for our iniquities; the punishment that brought us peace was upon him, and by his wounds we are healed" (Isa 53:4–5). Shalom is the priceless gift that we could never earn or deserve: "Therefore, since we have been justified through faith, we have peace with God through our Lord Jesus Christ . . ." (Rom 5:1).

Shalom embraces the fullness of salvation, which means deliverance from "sin and death; guilt and estrangement; ignorance of truth; bondage to habit and vice; fear of demons, of death, of life, of God, of hell; despair of self; alienation from others; pressures of the world; a meaningless life." The meaning of shalom is exceedingly positive, embracing "peace with God, access to God's favor and presence, hope of regaining the glory intended for humankind, endurance in suffering, steadfast character, an optimistic

---

2. Chambers, *My Utmost for His Highest*, December 19.

3. Quoted in Barth, *Dogmatics in Outline*, 151.

mind, inner motivations of divine love and power of the Spirit, ongoing experience of the risen Christ and sustaining joy in God."[4]

The peace we long for is the peace of God, for only his peace, "which transcends all understanding, will guard [our] hearts and [our] minds in Christ Jesus" (Phil 4:7). This is the lasting peace that survives the pain and suffering of this life and outlasts death itself. "You will keep in perfect peace him whose mind is steadfast, because he trusts in you. Trust in the Lord forever, for the Lord, the Lord himself, is the Rock eternal" (Isa 26:3–4).

Upper Room Reflection

How can a one word greeting, *shalom*, be the summation for salvation?

What is the significance of reading Jesus' admonition, "Let not your heart be troubled," as a command?

How is your longing for peace in the line with Jesus' gift of peace?

How do you experience the distinction between Christ's peace and worldly peace?

---

4. White, "Salvation," 968.

DAY 18

The Father is Greater than I

"You heard me say, 'I am going away and I am coming back to you.' If you loved me, you would be glad that I am going to the Father, for the Father is greater than I."

John 14:28

THE SPIRALING INTENSITY OF the upper room discourse continues with echoes from the opening theme (John 14:1). "You heard me say," reintroduces Jesus' definitive promise of the final Parousia, stated here in the first person singular with unambiguous clarity. Jesus assigns eschatological significance to his promise because all of his going and coming is from the Father. Sometimes we forget how much lies behind the shalom of God. Our existence is shaped by the fullness of the revelation of Jesus Christ. Christianity is impossible apart from Jesus' incarnation, crucifixion, resurrection, ascension, and second coming. The "progressive" modern version of Christianity that celebrates Jesus as a special human being, but not God in the flesh, is entirely false and misleading. Jesus made it very clear, "I am coming back to you." Without the ascension and the second coming there is no peace and comfort.

Surprisingly, Jesus emphasized the advantage of his leaving, both for himself and for his followers. "If you loved me, you would be glad that I am going to the Father, for the Father is greater than I." Jesus makes this personal. Disciples who truly love the risen Lord Jesus will want to see him ascend to the Father. Because of the timing of when he said this, there is a special pathos behind the conditional clause, "If you love me." Jesus has yet to experience Gethsemane's agony of soul, Judas's betrayal with a kiss, Peter's threefold denial, and the Father's abandonment on the cross because of our sin. Given all that Jesus went through on our behalf ("And being found in human form, he humbled himself and became obedient to the point of death—even death on a cross" [Phil 2:8]), wouldn't a true sign of our love for Christ be our desire for his exaltation and glorification? The long night of his earthly ministry is over. The incarnate one truly deserves to be reunited with the Father in glory. As John said in his introduction to the upper room, "Jesus knew that the hour had come for him to leave this world and go to the Father. . . . Jesus knew that the Father had put all things under his power, and that he had come from God and was returning to God . . ." (John 13:1, 3).

We are not surprised by the fact that Jesus wants the best for us, even though at times we may need convincing. The Apostle Paul reminds us, "He who did not spare his own Son, but gave him up for us all—how will he not also, along with him, graciously give us all things?" (Rom 8:32). But what may be surprising to us is that Jesus should want us to want the best for him. "If you love me, you would be glad that I am going to the Father." Love always seeks the best for the other, and that holds true even when we are referring to the second member of the Trinity. To love Christ for Christ's sake is the measure of our love for Christ. Children thrive best on their parents' sacrificial love but only when children learn to want the best for their parents, as their parents do for them, do they truly know the meaning of love.

The true meaning of the incarnation continues to surprise us, namely, that what we think about Jesus going to the Father after achieving our salvation really matters to Jesus. Our inclination may be to deny such an emotional longing in Jesus, but in the upper room Jesus made it clear that true devotion shares in Jesus' home-going joy. In less than twenty-four hours Jesus will be nailed to the cross. Jesus wants the disciples to be glad that he is going to the Father. "If you love me, you'll be glad." Jesus wasn't impressed with Middle Eastern grieving customs. What Jesus said to his disciples, we ought to say to one another. Death, "even death on a cross," does not end all. To our grieving loved ones we can say, "If you loved me, you would be glad that I am going to the Father." Our humanism rejoices that a loved one's suffering is over; but it is our devotion to Christ and our real hope that rejoices that our loved one is going to the Father.

We should be glad that Jesus has gone to the Father for his sake and for ours. We have two good reasons for rejoicing that the risen Lord Jesus has ascended to the Father. The second reason refers back to what Jesus said moments ago in the upper room: "Very truly I tell you, whoever believes in me will do the works I have been doing, and they will do even greater works than these, *because I am going to the Father*" (John 14:12). As we said what makes these works greater is the eschatological fulfillment of the risen Lord Jesus. Greater works will abound when the limitations of Jesus' incarnate earthly ministry are overcome in the ascension and Pentecost. The contrast is not between what Jesus did and what believers can do, but between Jesus' pre-exaltation ministry and his rule and reign at the right hand of the Father.

When Jesus says "the Father is greater than I am," he is comparing his self-emptying humility to the transcendent glory and majesty of the Father. His self-description is in keeping with his earthly ministry. Jesus is not claiming to be in any way inferior to the Father. He has testified to his complete oneness with the Father (John 10:30). Out of this Trinitarian oneness, Jesus chose to subordinate himself to the will of the Father. He became human for the sake of his mission to the world. But now the hour has come for him to return to the Father. Jesus refers to this shared glory in his high priestly prayer when he says, "And now, Father, glorify me in your presence with the glory I had with you before the world began" (John 17:5).

An early fourth-century Alexandrian priest by the name of Arius claimed that Jesus' statement was an acknowledgment by Jesus that he was not fully God. Arius argued that in his essential being, Jesus was subordinate to God and not equal with God.

There were times in the fourth century when it looked as though Arianism might triumph in the church, but in the end, the truth of the Son's essential oneness with the Father prevailed. The Nicean creed was formulated at the first ecumenical council in the history of the church. Over three hundred bishops met in AD 325. They affirmed the deity of Jesus Christ and refuted Arianism:

> We believe . . . in one Lord Jesus Christ, the Son of God, begotten from the Father, only-begotten, that is, from the substance of the Father, . . . begotten not made, of one substance with the Father . . . But as for those who say, There was when He was not, and before being born He was not, and that He came into existence out of nothing, or who assert that the Son of God is from a different . . . substance, or is created, or is subject to alteration or change—these the Catholic [i.e., universal] Church anathematizes.[1]

Disciples who love Jesus rejoice that he has gone to prepare a place for us. Jesus is with the Father, not only for his glory, but for our benefit. He will come again and take us to be where he is. Until then, we obey his command, "Do not let your hearts be troubled and do not be afraid."

Upper Room Reflection

Why does our love for Jesus' home-going matter to Jesus?

What is the evidence of that love?

How can we be glad over the death of the saints?

How does Jesus' upper room conversation shape your understanding of God?

---

1. Kelly, *Early Christian Doctrines*, 232.

DAY 19

Jesus' Disciple-Making Strategy

"I have told you now before it happens, so that
when it does happen you will believe. I will not
say much more to you . . ."

John 14:29–30

JESUS BRINGS CLOSURE TO his discipleship sermon in a manner consistent with the purpose of John's gospel: "But these are written that you may believe that Jesus is the Messiah, the Son of God, and that by believing you may have life in his name" (John 20:31). One of Jesus' disciple-making strategies is to give us a heads up on what to expect. He gets out in front of history, so his disciples are not blindsided by what's coming next. In the immediate context, his concluding comment refers back to his prediction of his betrayal: "I am telling you now before it happens, so that when it does happen you will believe that I am who I am" (John 13:19). But in the larger context, this communicational strategy underscores Jesus' entire ministry. He wants his disciples to know "the Master's business" (John 15:15). Jesus seeks to make believers out of us by giving spiritual direction that meets our future needs.

This impulse to prepare others ought to be shared by Jesus' followers. As parents, friends, pastors, and spouses, we have a responsibility to get out in front the world's challenges with teaching that helps believers believe. We should probably do a better job preparing believers for entering university. Parents, pastors, and youth ministers need to be able to say with Jesus, "I have told you all this now before it happens, so that when it happens you will believe." This could also be said about preparing people for marriage, for work, for suffering, for aging. We need to take the truth of the gospel seriously enough to get out in front of life's challenges.

Christ's followers take Jesus' pedagogical strategy to heart and model their teaching after the master. We cannot predict the future, but we can give spiritual direction that meets the challenges of the future. Because of what Jesus taught we can get out in front of history. We can offer the comfort and challenge that he offered in the upper room. His entire discourse is a case study in spiritual direction. We learn that betrayal and denial are always pending realities, that new commandment love shapes our lives, and that Jesus is the way, the truth, and the life. The church is entrusted with a message that goes well beyond the cliché "Jesus saves." Christ's disciples partner with the Spirit of truth to explain the goings and comings of Jesus: the Parousia, the Passion, the Paraclete, and the Presence. Yes, it is a whole lot to believe! But then, there is no excuse for dumbing down of the gospel. A "minimal Jesus" makes believers vulnerable to a host of problems and temptations. Substantive reasons are needed to develop resilient saints. When the church says, "Do not let your hearts be troubled," believers have to know why they can let the peace of Christ rule in their hearts (John 14:1; Col 3:15). We are charged to teach the whole counsel of God.

Once again the pressing circumstances of the devil's attack are in view when Jesus says, "I will not say much more to you, for the prince of this world is coming." But the lesson to be drawn is greater than the immediate circumstances of the upper room. All good teaching is overshadowed by an inescapable evil. The gospel doesn't exist in a spiritual vacuum. There is no neutral zone, free of demonic challenge. True spiritual direction is always delivered on the world's turf and confronted by life-threatening conditions that require urgent care. Academic posturing and preaching performances are out of place in the upper room. There is little time or patience for idle curiosity and abstract sophistry. That said, evil never dictates the tone or timing of Jesus' teaching. There is no panic or anger in Jesus' voice, and neither should there be in ours. We are dependent upon the Spirit of God and the Word of God. The recipients of our spiritual direction should be assured that they are receiving what they need to know to follow Christ.

All good teaching requires a cycle of instruction and application. Listening to the voice of Jesus leads to action: meaning and mission are inseparable. "I will not say much more to you" signals that Jesus' discipleship sermon is coming to a conclusion and that his spiritual direction is about to be put to the test. We would like the intimacy, if not the security, of the upper room to last forever, but it cannot. The mission of God lies outside the upper room. The four major goings and comings of Jesus make it possible for us to move out into the world to "make disciples of all nations, baptizing them in the name of the Father and of the Son and of the Holy Spirit, and teaching them to obey everything I have commanded you" (Matt 28:19–20). Jesus' teaching is centripetal, compelling us to center our lives in him and his teaching, but it is also centrifugal, moving us out into the world "because God so loved the world that he gave his one and only Son" (John 3:16).

Upper Room Reflection

Identify a particular struggle that you wish you were better prepared for.

What are the ways that we can help ourselves and other believers become more resilient?

Why is the church obligated to teach more than "Jesus saves"?

Why can't the Christian life be lived exclusively in the upper room?

DAY 20

The Ruler of This World

" . . . For the ruler of this world is coming. He has no
hold over me, but he comes so that the world may learn
that I love the Father and do exactly what my Father
has commanded me."

John 14:30–31

THE MISSION OF GOD and the dominion of the world are on a col-
lision course. This is how it has been and will continue to be until
God brings evil to an end. And the end of evil will not come about
through legal reform or advances in education or a thriving global
economy or international efforts for world peace. Evil will only
come to an end in God's final judgment. The will to power and
the weapons of this world will not achieve the end of evil, only its
advance. The ruler of this world keeps coming and coming, doing
everything in his power to overcome the good.

Jesus is experienced in the devil's coming and goings. From the
moment he was born the devil was out to get him. The devil's strategy was behind Herod's Gestapo-type raid on Bethlehem slaugh-
tering the innocents (Matt 2:16–18). The devil came to Jesus in the
wilderness when he led Jesus "to a very high mountain and showed
him all the kingdoms of the world and their splendor. 'All this I will
give you,' he said, 'if you will bow down and worship me.' Jesus said
to him, 'Away from me, Satan! For it is written: Worship the Lord
your God, and serve him only'" (Matt 4:8–10). The devil came to
Jesus in the form of an angry mob threatening to stone him because

Jesus said, "I and the Father are one." The devil came to Jesus in Judas's betrayal and in Peter's denial. He was there in the Sanhedrin's deliberations and he took a front-row seat when Pilate washed his hands of justice. The devil came to Jesus at the cross and danced a short-lived victory dance. From birth to death, the devil kept coming, seeking to devour the one who came to bring salvation.

On the subject of the devil the Bible gives us enough information to be on guard, but not enough to indulge our curiosity. Markus Barth observes, "Though [the devil] is often mentioned in the Bible, it is impossible to derive an ontology, phenomenology, and history of Satan sufficiently complete to create a 'satanology' which in the slightest measure corresponds to the weight of biblical 'theo-logy.'"[1] We were meant to be aware of the devil and the power of evil, but never engrossed in the subject. For example, no one need be a student of pornography to be on guard against pornography. To dwell on pornography would be to become its victim. Likewise with the devil, demonic power is real, but should not be fixated on. C. S. Lewis strikes the balance between insight and scorn in *The Screwtape Letters*, his literary exposé of covert demonic temptation. Lewis quoted Martin Luther's line and then followed it: "The best way to drive out the devil, if he will not yield to text of Scripture, is to jeer and flout him, for he cannot bear scorn."[2] The spirit of the antichrist pervades the world but as John reminds us, "Greater is he that is in you than he that is in the world" (1 John 4:4).

Jesus' description of the devil as "the ruler of the world" concedes nothing to the devil but the fact of his demonic existence and his hell-bent determination to rule the world. Jesus is taking his "stand against the devil's schemes" (Eph 6:11). To recognize "the devil's schemes" is to see the world from God's perspective. The forces of evil behind man's inhumanity to man defy human explanation. There is a demonic source and energy behind atrocities and catastrophes. Human culpability plus demonic activity

1. Barth, *Ephesians*, 228.
2. Lewis, *The Screwtape Letters*, vii.

magnifies and compounds evil beyond human calculation. I am speaking here of such evils as genocide, the sex-slave industry, the brainwashed child warriors of Uganda, witchcraft and animism, and the ideological captivity of the West. There is a demonic twist to nature-alone scientism and the nihilistic dismissal of salvation history. The war on terrorism reminds us that we are in the war to end all wars, because this war will not end until Christ comes again. Jesus underscored the power behind the power when he spoke to Pilate. "You would have no power over me if it were not given to you from above. Therefore the one who handed me over to you is guilty of a greater sin" (John 19:11). Knowing the enemy behind our enemies helps us to respond to others the way Jesus did.

Jesus is not intimidated by the devil, because the devil has no hold over him. Evil has no leverage where there is no sin. Simple obedience to the Father's will defeats the devil's false accusations and lies. In Hebrew Satan means "adversary" and there is no denying that he is a formidable enemy. Peter describes the devil as a roaring lion on the prowl looking for prey. But Peter also gave this straightforward spiritual direction: "Resist him, standing firm in the faith, because you know that the family of believers, throughout the world is undergoing the same kind of sufferings" (1 Pet 5:9). Loving obedience to the will of the Father through the costly grace of Christ robs evil of its power.

Not only do the devil's schemes have no hold on Jesus, the devil's anticipated victory at the cross backfires. Instead of defeating Christ once and for all, the devil's actions only serve to set up the ultimate faithfulness test that Jesus passes with flying colors. Inadvertently "the god of this age" helps the world see the full extent of God's love, the giving of his one and only Son (2 Cor 4:4; John 3:16). Like so many tyrants throughout history, the ruler of this world wants to bring the world down with him, but Jesus lays down his life for the world in loving obedience to the Father (John 10:17–18). The world is the devil's terrain. "Enemy-occupied territory—that is what the world is," wrote C. S. Lewis. But "Christianity is the story of how the rightful king has landed, you might say in disguise, and is calling us all to take part in a great campaign of sabotage."[3]

> "And the God of all grace, who called you to his eternal glory in Christ, after you have suffered a little while, will himself restore you and make you strong, firm and steadfast. To him be the power for ever and ever. Amen" (1 Pet 5:10–11).

Upper Room Reflection

Why was it important to acknowledge the devil at the beginning and at the end of the upper room discourse (John 13:2; 14:30)?

What can we learn from Jesus's designation of the devil as the ruler of the world?

How do we strike a balance between awareness of the devil's power and giving the devil too much attention?

Has there ever been a time in your life when God turned the devil's triumph into the devil's defeat?

3. Lewis, *Mere Christianity*, 46.

DAY 21

Move Out!

"Get up, let's get out of here!"

John 14:31

IF JESUS FOCUSES ON his four big comings—the Parousia, the Paraclete, the Passion, and his abiding Presence—why does John bother about this little getting up and going? The scene changes abruptly and seems to interrupt Jesus' spiritual direction and prayer. Some have conjectured that there were two versions of the upper room discourse (John 13:1–14:30; 15:1–17:26). Another speculative idea is that "Come now; let us leave" belongs at the end of chapter 17. The simplest solution is probably the best: Jesus concluded their time in the upper room and the band of disciples headed out. They walked through the narrow streets of Jerusalem, past the temple, toward the garden of Gethsemane. They didn't actually leave the old city and cross the Kidron Valley until Jesus finished praying (John 18:1).

Jesus' earthy "Let's get out of here!" underscores the sufficiency of his spiritual direction. Even if nothing more was said the disciples were on solid ground for hope. Perhaps Jesus chose these "secular words of departure" instead of a benediction to highlight the real-world impact of mission of God.[1] There is something impressive about his matter-of-fact tone. The conversation continues even as the real work commences. Jesus' teaching resists spiritualization. His meaning cannot be sustained in isolation from the

1. Bruner, *John*, 851.

78

ensuing conflict with evil and the triumph of the cross. I find the words, "Come now; let us leave," compelling because they challenge my sinful tendency to stay safe and secure in the upper room.

I picture the twelve, now eleven, just trying to keep up with Jesus, who for his part was neither busy nor bored, but always on the move. And his movement was always redemptive, moving toward the cross. Jesus lived in sync with the Father's *kairos* timing, infusing each moment with the movement of salvation history. When he talked to the Samaritan woman, it was as if heaven and earth converged at Jacob's well. When he preached the Sermon on the Mount, he was God incarnate transposing the law into the key of grace.

There are two Greek words for time. *Chronos* measures the existence of time. It keeps tabs on the length of time. *Kairos* measures the essence of time—grace-filled time. Jesus introduced *kairos* time in Nazareth at the start of his public ministry. He said, "The time has come. The Kingdom of God is near. Repent and believe the good news!"(Mark 1:15). This *kairos* timing was true of Jesus' goings and comings every day of his earthly ministry. To keep up with Jesus meant living in the Father's *kairos* time zone. When Jesus said "let's go" the disciples had the good sense to follow. Who in their right mind would want to be left out?

Jesus' matter-of-fact departure underscores the synergy of his message and mission. Good teaching is closely linked to the daily task of taking up our cross and following Jesus. Discipleship is a real-world apprenticeship, not an academic exercise. The departure is paradigmatic of the fact that the sent one goes along with those who are sent. The God who comforts continues to reassure the disciples with his real presence. We are not alone. God keeps his promise: "And surely I am with you always, to the very end of the age" (Matt 28:20). Jesus' spiraling conversation on fruitfulness, friendship, and faithfulness was exactly what the disciples needed heading into to the next twenty-four hours. It is exactly what we need.

comfort in times of confusion and uncertainty

Upper Room Reflection

Why is it important that Jesus' spiritual direction continues after the disciples leave the upper room?

How good are you at keeping up with Jesus?

Explain the distinction between *chronos* and *kairos* timing in your life.

How can you cultivate the presence of Christ in your daily routine?

DAY 22

The True Vine

"I am the true vine, and my Father is the gardener."

John 15:1

THE CONVERSATION ALONG THE way flows so naturally from the upper room discourse that there is no need to separate them. "Let's move out" changes the venue not the vision. Streetwise spiritual direction is consistent with the table fellowship of the upper room. Three days from now Jesus will have another extended conversation. Only this time the risen Jesus will be on road to Emmaus explaining "what was said in all the Scriptures concerning himself" (Luke 24:27). Throughout his earthly ministry Jesus used the physical journey as a stage for the spiritual journey. His pedagogical style was not limited to sacred spaces and religious times. The real presence of God pervaded the everyday world. He turned the ordinary routine into an occasion for spiritual direction. We remember Moses instructing the people to talk about the commandments "when you sit at home and when you walk along the road" (Deut 6:7). True spirituality spills over into everyday life, because its truest expression is in the ordinary social setting. The feet that Jesus had washed were no longer clean but the cleansing truth of Jesus continued as they walked toward the Kidron Valley.

On the way Jesus and the disciples may have passed by the Temple. Above the gate in stone relief were golden vines with grape clusters as big as a man. The evening shadows may have obscured the image, but Jesus' metaphor invoked deep biblical roots. The vine was the iconic symbol of Israel, used by the prophets to indict Israel. Hosea charged that even though God made Israel fruitful she persisted in worshiping other gods (Hos 10:1–2). Isaiah declared, "The vineyard of the Lord Almighty is the nation of Israel" (Isa 5:7). On a fertile hillside, Yahweh planted only the choice vines and did everything possible to care for his crop, but his vine only produced bad fruit (Isa 2:1–7). Jeremiah accused this "choice vine" of becoming "a corrupt, wild vine" (Jer 2:21). Ezekiel likened Israel to a useless vine and lamented that wood from a vine was good for nothing but to be burned (Ezek 15:1–5).

The psalmist used the vine to tell the story of Israel from Exodus to judgment: "You transplanted a vine from Egypt; you drove out the nations and planted it. . . . Your vine is cut down, it is burned with fire; at your rebuke your people perish." But then the psalmist unexpectedly shifts the focus from the depressing story of the vine to the messianic hope of the Son of Man. "Let your hand rest on the man at your right hand, the son of man you have raised up for yourself" (Ps 80:8–17). The indictment of the prophets and the hope of the psalmist is answered in the one who says, "I am the true vine" (John 15:1). This is the seventh and final "I am" saying of Jesus in the Gospel of John.[1] Jesus used descriptive images drawn from the Bible to paint a messianic self-portrait free from nationalistic and political triumph. The comparison is straightforward: Israel is the false vine, Jesus is the true vine.

The metaphor of the vine invokes self-scrutiny. Our connections apart from God proliferate in our hectic lives at the expense of being grounded in Christ. Our fallen human condition predisposes us to find "community" outside of Jesus in any number of competing networks. We are not naturally inclined to find in Jesus the root of the matter. We are often more at home with the little trinity of me, myself, and I than we are with the holy Trinity. To be honest, we might sooner say, "I am the true vine and Jesus is the

---

1. The other "I am" sayings include: "I am the bread of life" (6:35); "I am the light of the world" (8:12); "I am the gate of the sheep" (10:7); "I am the good shepherd" (10:11); "I am the resurrection and the life" (11:25); and "I am the way and the truth and the life" (14:6).

branch." But if Jesus is the branch and we are the vine we abide in a Christ-less Christianity. The prophets used the image of the vine to indict Israel, but Jesus used the image to comfort his disciples. Jesus invites us—his followers—to be rooted and grounded in him, to be at home with him.

Upper Room Reflection

How do you picture the disciples listening to Jesus' spiritual direction? Where and when are you most receptive to spiritual direction?

What is the significance of Jesus being the true vine and Israel being the false vine?

How do we counter the notion, "I am the vine and Jesus is the branch"?

How does Jesus' conversation on the way echo themes already stated in the upper room?

DAY 23

Organic Spirituality

"I am the true vine, and my Father is the gardener."

John 15:1

THE IMAGERY OF THE vine underscores the believer's path to discipleship. The Bible has plenty of "visual aids" that instruct us in what it means to be at home with Jesus. Like the easy yoke or the towel and the basin or the Apostle Paul's jars of clay metaphor, these images help us to visualize the meaning of discipleship. They serve as object lessons of instruction, appealing to our praying imagination in order to shape our understanding of what it means to follow Jesus.

The vine symbolizes God's initiative and our surrender. Disciples yield to the will of God the way a plant yields to forces of nature. The image captures the inner logic of how Christians grow up in the faith. Instead of feeling the pressure to make something of ourselves, the metaphor underscores our willed passivity, our submission to the Father's will. We cannot manufacture fruitfulness, but we can abide in the one who produces fruit.

Our failure to grasp this picture of organic spirituality often leads to artificial efforts to jump-start a "deeper life." Well-intentioned guides come up with programs and techniques that promise renewal. Stages of spiritual growth are plotted and a spiritual to-do list is drawn up. Try as we might, we cannot seem to get the picture of soul-satisfying discipleship in focus. We give ourselves a pep talk and eagerly look for a five-step formula for spiritual growth. But the DNA for authentic discipleship is not the will to perform but the discipline of surrender. We grow in Christ when we are obedient to his commands, open to his love, receptive of his discipline, committed to his mission, and resting in his will. Willed passivity is anything but a cop-out; it is an intentional act of devotion founded on the grace of Christ that requires every fiber of our being.

After celebrating the Last Supper, Jesus linked the blood of the covenant (the cup) to the ultimate eschatological fulfillment in the Father's kingdom (the fruit of the vine). "I tell you," Jesus said, "I will not drink from this fruit of the vine from now on until that day when I drink it new with you in my Father's kingdom" (Matt 26:29). Taken all together Jesus merged three great realities out of true vine imagery: the atonement, the second coming, and the believer's union in Christ. He alone is the true embodiment of Israel and the hope of the world. The metaphor of the vine spans the full scope of salvation and underscores the natural indwelling of the incarnation and discipleship.

Jesus likens himself to the true vine and the Father to a farmer or a "husbandman" or an "orchardist." The image of God in blue jeans clearing stones, planting choice vines, tending his vineyard, and preparing in advance for a crop of good grapes fits perfectly with the purpose and mission of the incarnation. Father and Son are in this together. The Father sends his Son: "For God so loved the world that he gave his one and only Son . . ." (John 3:16). The Son submits to the Father's will: "Who, being in very nature God, did not consider equality with God something to be used to his own advantage; rather made himself nothing by taking the very nature of a servant . . ." (Phil 2:6–7). Jesus adds to this Trinitarian description when he promises to send the Spirit of truth (John 15:26).

Since Jesus is the true vine and God the Father is the gardener there is little left for us to worry about. Everything has been taken care of. Our place is secure. We are rooted in the true source of abundant life and fruitfulness. Disciples are invited to rest under the sovereign care of our heavenly Father and live into the nurturing reality of God's redemptive and sanctifying provision.

The humanizing and practical element of this organic spirituality is vividly portrayed in these down-to-earth images of a fruitful vine and a caring gardener. What Jesus is saying here is that true spirituality is homemade. There is nothing artificial or contrived about it. It resonates with the inscape of our souls and the landscape of our mission. Jesus gives foot-washing clarity to his spiritual direction: remain in the vine and rest in the care of the gardener. That's all we really need to know.

Upper Room Reflection

How does Jesus' imagery of the vine help you understand the Christian life?

Does Jesus' picture of true spirituality resonate with what you have been taught about spirituality?

What does it mean for Jesus to say "my Father is the gardener"?

How does the vine metaphor help us to grasp the meaning of willed passivity?

Cutting Off and Cleaning Up

"He cuts off every branch in me that bears no fruit,
while every branch that does bear fruit he prunes so
that it will be even more fruitful. You are already
clean because of the word I have spoken to you."

John 15:2–3

FRUITFUL VINES NEED CONSTANT care. The gardener cuts off the
dead branches and cuts back the unwanted shoots from fruitful
branches. In Greek all three words, cutting off (*airei*), cutting back
(*kath-airei*), and cleansing (*katharoi*) are related etymologically.
From the Greek we get such English words as catharsis, cathartic,
as well as the name Catharine ("pure").[1] The health and purity of
the vine is preserved by severing the dead wood and trimming the
good branches. But Jesus quickly moves beyond the horticulturist
image and underscores the cleansing and purifying power of the
Word. Earlier in the upper room Jesus assured the disciples that
they were clean (*katharos*). "Those who have had a bath," Jesus
said, "need only to wash their feet; their whole body is clean" (John
13:10). Vine trimming and bathing point to the same reality: God's
word cleanses and purifies.

We may be startled to read that the Father "cuts off every
branch in me that bears no fruit." We are disturbed to find that
these diseased branches are in Christ. External religion alone offers no assurance of salvation. We recall the man in Jesus' parable

1. Bruner, *John*, 879.

of the Wedding Banquet, who came to the wedding in his old
work clothes (Matt 22:1–14). We can be baptized, regular church
attenders, and attentive to sermons, but in the absence of life-
changing saving faith we are just going through the motions. We
can embrace the ritual and the tradition and cultivate a religious
habit, yet not know Christ. Make-believe Christians are dead
wood. Judas is our prime example of being close to Jesus but as
far removed from real faith and trust in Christ as a person can be.
Judas died on the vine.

There is a tension in the Gospel of John between deep and
lasting assurance and a soul-searching warning. It is *always* possible for disciples *including me* to call it quits. When Jesus said,
"Very truly I tell you, unless you eat the flesh of the Son of Man
and drink his blood, you have no life in you," many of his disciples
said in effect, "We're out of here" (John 6:53, 60). The possibility
of rejection must be weighed against Jesus' strong words of assurance: "And this is the will of him who sent me, that I shall lose
none of all those he has given me, but raise them up at the last day"
(John 6:39). He promised categorically that his "sheep" listen to his
voice and "they shall never perish; no one will snatch them out of
my hand" (John 10:28).

We may not want to take Jesus' warning seriously and personally, but we should. We might wish that the author of Hebrews
rephrased his warning against falling away differently. Why didn't
he say that it is *impossible* for those "who have tasted the heavenly
gift" to fall away? Instead, he said that it is impossible for those
"who have shared in the Holy Spirit, who have tasted the goodness
of the word of God and the powers of the coming age, and who
have fallen away, to be brought back to repentance" (Heb 6:4–6).

No one should ever hear this warning and say, "I can't come
back to Christ because I fell away and Hebrews tells me that it is
impossible for me to return to Christ." Let it be emphasized that
this is not what Hebrews is saying. Christ's gospel always remains
good news to the lost—always! What the author of Hebrews is
warning against is the hardness of heart and the resistance of will
that humanly speaking makes repentance impossible. Familiarity

with the benefits of Christ can breed an antichrist contempt for the gospel that despises the sacrifice of Christ. John helps resolve the tension between assurance and warning in his letter when he says, "They went out from us, but they did not really belong to us. For if they had belonged to us, they would have remained with us; but their going showed that none of them belonged to us. But you have an anointing from the Holy One, and all of you know the truth" (1 John 2:19–20).

Jesus' reference to severing dead branches was not meant to arouse anxiety among the disciples. He quickly reassures them, saying, "You are already clean because of the word I have spoken to you" (John 15:3). His intention was for all disciples to understand the fruit-bearing necessity of real faithfulness. The gardener's work is never done. The word of God trims, cleans, and purifies our lives. The Spirit of truth is on the job applying the gospel in fresh ways, cutting back all those ideas, traits, and actions that do not fit with the gospel of Christ so that we might produce more fruit.

If Judas is a prime example of cutting off the dead branch, Peter is a prime example of the Father's pruning, purifying, and sanctifying work. We can identify with Peter and recognize our need for cutting back our willful ways and our wrong-headed action. Human flourishing requires the Father's gardening skills. I am not a gardener and I don't know much about keeping trees healthy, so when our ivy tree grew scrawny and bare, I Googled what to do. For months I tried watering and fertilizing but nothing worked. Finally, with a degree of trepidation, I cut it way back and waited. At least one of my neighbors thought I had killed it. I contemplated the embarrassment of cutting it down and removing the stump, but happily, my ivy tree came back to life. The leaves are thick and dark green and the tree looks better than ever. I may not like to admit it, but like my ivy tree I need constant trimming. Bruner writes, "Something comparably miraculous and fruitful waits on the other side of every faithful disciple's prunings and crosses."[2]

2. Ibid., 880.

Upper Room Reflection

How does the Word of God cleanse Christ's followers?

Describe your experience of God's pruning.

What does becoming more fruitful involve in your life?

How can we encourage one another in this pruning process?

DAY 25

Living into Jesus

"Live in me. Make your home in me just as I do in you. In the same way that a branch can't bear grapes by itself but only by being joined to the vine, you can't bear fruit unless you are joined with me."

John 15:4 (The Message)

JESUS KNEW THAT HIS disciples were about to be plunged into chaos. Following his arrest in the garden of Gethsemane, his disciples fled the scene (Matt 26:56). But the pressure of this unfolding drama sharpens Jesus' personal appeal for continued deep fellowship with his disciples. His selfless spiritual direction is unaffected by the imminent danger. He continues his reassuring message of comfort. The disciples will feel like homeless refugees, like fugitives on the run, but Jesus is intent on inviting them to make their home with him.

Humanly speaking, Jesus' conversation on the way seems incongruous. A tense silence as his entourage made its way to the Kidron Valley would have better suited the circumstances. Everything that Jesus stood for and worked to achieve appears to be coming to a violent end, yet Jesus insists on making an intimate appeal for continued friendship. "Stick with me," he says, just before he is arrested and accused of blasphemy before the Sanhedrin. "Make your home with me" is his last message before being charged with treason and sedition. "If you want to be fruitful stay connected to me" is his personal plea on the eve of his crucifixion. The intensity of the moment and the timing and tenor of his spiritual direction is remarkable.

If Jesus was anyone else, we would say he was living in denial. The religious and political authorities must have thought he was either delusional or devious. His disciples were confused. In the upper room Jesus said, "Where I am going, you cannot come" (John 13:33). He explained, "I am going . . . and if I go and prepare a place for you, I will come back and take you to be with me" (John 14:2–3). But now he is insisting that they remain in him—that they make their home with him.

The disciples' questions have ceased and Jesus' monologue proceeds uninterrupted. He is streaming live into the confused minds of emotionally exhausted disciples who want to hear everything Jesus has to say, but who are struggling to keep up with what he means. Jesus' easy metaphor of the vine and his simple descriptive words belie the profound meaning he expects his disciples to grasp. With that said, Jesus doesn't appear to be overly concerned about them "getting it." Building toward understanding is a process that at times is slow and painful, but it has to begin somewhere. Jesus refused to be intimidated by the circumstances and turned what might have been a silent walk of doom into a beautiful invitation along the way. Jesus knew that this was more than they could bear, but his timing was perfect. If the disciples only picked up his comforting tone that was enough.

On the eve of his separation from the disciples, Jesus' invitation to "remain in me" is best understood in the light of his teaching from the beginning.[1] Jesus has stayed on message throughout his earthly ministry. The theme of living into Jesus or making our home with Jesus has been there from the very first encounter when the disciples asked, "where are you staying?" (John 1:37). The same Greek word *menein* is used in both contexts. Jesus responded to the disciples' question, "Rabbi, where are you making your home?" by saying, "Come and see." And they did. They went and saw where he was staying and they "made their home with Jesus here

1. Bruner, *John*, 881–83.

by wanting to be with him."[2] The word to *remain* or *abide* or *make our home* with Jesus grows in significance until it climaxes in John 15. The disciples' initial question is followed up in the end by Jesus taking the initiative and inviting his disciples to make their home with him.

The same Greek work is used when the Samaritan village responded to the testimony of the woman at the well and invited Jesus to make his home with them (*meinai*) (John 4:40). The home-making word (*meinai*) is used again in John 6:56, when Jesus says, "Whoever eats my flesh and drinks my blood remains in me, and I in them." Holy Communion is the key for making our home with Jesus. Jesus used the word *meinai* again when he said, "If you hold to my teaching (or, if you make your home in my Word), you are really my disciples. Then you will know the truth, and the truth will set you free" (John 8:31–32). The theme of making our home with Jesus has been growing right from the beginning of the Gospel.

Second, Jesus' appeal to "Remain in me" brings to a conclusion his fourfold emphasis on his goings and comings. The final Parousia, the Resurrection Passion, the gift of the Paraclete, and his abiding Presence define the multiple ways God in Christ makes himself real to us. Throughout John 14 Christ promises his presence *in the future* ("I will come back and take you to be with me"), *in the present* (". . . the world will not see me anymore, but you will see me. Because I live, you also will live"), *in the gift of the Spirit* ("I will ask the Father, and he will give you another advocate to help you and be with you forever—the Spirit of truth"), and *in his faithful presence* ("Remain in me, as I remain in you").

Third, the Spirit of truth will help us understand what it means to make our home with Jesus. The Holy Spirit, the Paraclete, will make sure that this deeply personal invitation to live into Jesus will be remembered and understood not only by the disciples walking the streets of Jerusalem that night, but by all disciples. Jesus was fully aware of the pending crisis and the conflicted emotions of the disciples. But he gave this spiritual direction in the confidence

---

2. Ibid., 882.

that the Holy Spirit would guide the disciples "into all truth" (John 16:13). Jesus' message of comfort, like all good spiritual direction, relies on the whole message of the gospel, the eschatological reality of Christ's goings and comings, and on the selfless work of the Spirit of truth who "will speak only what he hears, and he will tell you what is yet to come."

The verb "to remain" is used eleven times to emphasize the importance of making our home with Jesus (John 15:4–10).[3] Ten times the verb "to remain" is used positively. The only negative occurrence is in the middle: "If you do not remain in me, you are like a branch that is thrown away . . ." The ratio between positive and negative admonition is ten to one. Jesus reiterates ten times over the positive value of what it means to remain in his love. You would think we would get the message!

Upper Room Reflection

Reflect on the distractions that make it difficult for us to embrace Jesus' message.

What does it mean to you to remain in Jesus?

What steps can you take to live into Jesus?

How has God helped us to abide in him?

3. In our English translations of John 15:4 the second occurrence of "remain" is implicit in the Greek: "Remain in me, as I also remain in you."

DAY 26

Fruitful

"I am the vine; you are the branches. If you remain in me and I in you, you will bear much fruit; apart from me you can do nothing. If you do not remain in me, you are like a branch that is thrown away and withers; such branches are picked up, thrown into the fire and burned."

John 15:5–6

THE PRODUCTIVE LIFE ROOTED in Jesus is very different from the successful life dependent on the world. Sometimes they overlap and the believer is fruitful in the eyes of God and successful in the eyes of the world, but this is more rare than we care to admit. Remaining in Jesus is a question of fidelity. To make our home with Jesus is to persist in the life of faith. It is a loyal steadfastness to Christ characterized by a continuous openness to all that God in Christ offers us.[1]

Jesus emphasizes once again that he alone is the true, authentic vine in opposition to all the false vines that vie for our devotion. There is only one true vine. What or who is our vine is the crucial question prompted by Jesus' conversation on the way to Gethsemane. Our setting is not the narrow streets of Jerusalem on the eve of the crucifixion, but it might as well be since everything is at stake for us just as it was for the first disciples. If our vine is

---

1. Bultmann, *John*, 535.

the world or some aspect of the world such as work or sports or adventure then Jesus is reduced to a branch stemming from our false source of worldly vitality and inspiration. If I have made myself the vine and Jesus a branch I may have only succeeded in obscuring my barrenness with some specious form of spirituality.

To remain in Jesus is a deeply personal experience but it is far more practical than it is mystical. The disciple's life is expressed in loving obedience and obedient love. *Abiding* does not mean fleeing the world or disengaging from the world, but rather being like Jesus in the world: faithful to the Father's will, compassionate to those in need, boldly prophetic to those who seek to manipulate the truth to their sinful advantage, and resting in the salvation that is by God's grace through faith and that not of ourselves, but the gift of God. Being fruitful is a simple matter of hearing and obeying: "See that what you have heard from the beginning remains in you. If it does, you also will remain in the Son and in the Father. And this is what he promised us—eternal life" (1 John 2:24).

There is no excuse for us to make discipleship into a mystery. The image of the vine implies resting in the provision of God. Jesus is the vine and the Father is the gardener. Fruitful productivity is the organic result of a humble dependence on the Lord Jesus in the midst of ordinary life. It is not the product of spirituality that calls attention to itself. The metaphor of the vine does not imply that we exist in a vegetative state unaware of our decisive responsibility to follow Jesus. Disciples are not plants, but ordinary people—bodies, minds, and souls in community—made in God's image with capacities for love and obedience. Sin has shriveled up these capacities but God's grace redeems our withered state and restores us to fruit-bearing productivity. We were dead branches good for nothing but for the fire (Ezek 15:3), but now in Christ we can be the "the real fruit of the vine, the life of Jesus reproduced in the midst of the life of the world."[2]

Faithfulness and fruitfulness are inseparable. To remain in Jesus means that we will naturally bear fruit and the only way we

2. Newbigin, *The Light Has Come*, 198.

can bear fruit is by remaining in Jesus. There is a vital synergy between making our home with Jesus and fulfilling our mission in the world. We cannot make our home with Jesus and not get up and get going when he says, "Let's move out." The faithful Christian can no more not produce fruit than a fruitful Christian can prove to be faithless. The unmistakable quality of all fruit-bearing disciples is a vital demonstration of faithfulness. Faithfulness is not summed up in righteous works nor is fruitfulness a record of accomplishments. It is not a tally of saved souls or years of service; it is more organic and personal than bottom-line statistics or a list of accomplishments. Both faithfulness and fruitfulness are resourced in an abiding personal relationship with Jesus Christ. From him and only from him we learn how to love obedience and practice obedient love.

Fruit is a perishable commodity and has only a short shelf life. Fresh fruit in season is the daily work of Christ's followers. It is the open-ended blessing of following Jesus today in all the relationships, challenges, opportunities, and responsibilities that today affords. All the while we rest in the willed passivity that is the absolute blessing of Jesus being the vine and the Father being the gardener.

Upper Room Reflection

Does your life reflect the reality that there is only one true vine?

How is fruitful productivity in Christ different from success in the world?

How has your church and family background influenced what it means to abide in Christ?

Do you agree that faithfulness and fruitfulness cannot be separated?

DAY 27

Whatever You Wish!

"If you remain in me and my words remain in you,
ask whatever you wish, and it will be done for you.
This is to my Father's glory, that you bear much
fruit, showing yourselves to be my disciples."

John 15:7–8

OUR REAL DESIRES ARE the measure of our at-home-ness with
Jesus. To remain in Jesus is to be immersed in his will and word.
Our hopes and dreams are inspired by his word. This is an organic
process that grows within us, generating a new nature and new desires, that we never would have apart from Christ. In prayer we step
out of our old nature with its inherently self-focused, self-serving,
and self-glorifying ways and we gradually and gladly enter into the
mission of God. Jesus' conversation on the way is commentary on
his new command: "Love one another. As I have loved you, so you
must love one. By this everyone will know that you are my disciples, if you love one another" (John 13:34–35). The proof of our
internal desires is found in the fresh fruit of our Christ-likeness.
If we make our home with Jesus, his words will find a home in us,
and we can ask for whatever we want and it's ours.[1]

Jesus' bold "whatever you wish" promise is based squarely on
the word of God. It is not a blank check to be spent on whatever
fancies us, but an invitation to engage in Christ's kingdom work.
This unqualified and absolute promise makes no sense cut off

1. Bruner, *John*, 899.

98

from the indwelling word of God. This is the word that prunes and purifies our desires so that we seek first Christ's kingdom and righteousness (Matt 6:33). Augustine used the promise to point to the Lord's Prayer and counseled, "Let us adhere to the words and the meaning of *this* prayer in our petitions, and [then] whatever we ask will be done for us."[2] The disciple's "whatever" prayer corresponds to the "greater works" wrought by the risen and ascended Lord Jesus. Jesus said, "I will do whatever you ask in my name, so that the Father may be glorified in the Son. You may ask anything in my name, and I will do it" (John 14:12–14). The key to believing in the promise of Jesus is praying in the name of Jesus. Our personal desires are shaped by the one in whose name we pray. We pray the way he taught us to pray and the way he himself prayed: "Yet not as I will, but as you will" (Matt 26:39).

This "whatever you wish" prayer is the polar opposite to our wish dreams. Most of us have to work through a painful process of disillusionment where our dreams of the good life clash with God's good and perfect will. We are more deeply conformed to this world and its desires than we realize. The renewing of our mind can be a slow process of transformation whereby we are led by the Spirit of truth into the meaning of God's word. Dietrich Bonhoeffer, the German pastor-theologian who stood up to Hitler said emphatically, "God hates visionary dreaming; it makes the dreamer proud and pretentious."[3] He recognized how self-righteously arrogant we can become in insisting on our own way and imposing our agenda on others—all in the name of Jesus.

Fruitful disciples have the dual impact of bringing glory to the Father and showing the world that they belong to Jesus Christ. The theme of glory runs through Jesus' passion narrative from foot-washing to the cross. The glory of God is defined in the light of the cross. Jesus said, "The hour has come for the Son of Man to be glorified. Very truly I tell you, unless a kernel of wheat falls to the ground and dies, it remains only a single seed. . . . Now, my

2. Ibid.
3. Bonhoeffer, *Life Together*, 27.

soul is troubled, and what shall I say? 'Father, save me from this hour'? No, it was for this reason I came to this hour. Father, glorify your name!" (John 12:23–27). There is no other way to bring glory to the Father than to follow the pattern of self-sacrificing service given to us by Jesus. As we said earlier in our reflection on John 13, when the glory of God is co-opted by visions of worldly power and personal success it is yanked from its biblical roots and severed from its tie to the humility of the cross. God answers our "whatever-we-wish" prayers in keeping with his word, for the sake of his glory, and to make us more fruitful.

Fruit-bearing disciples show the world that they belong to Jesus Christ. They are Beatitude-based believers with salt and light impact. Their heart righteousness is visible to the world in practical, costly obedience. They practice the spiritual disciplines of prayer, giving, and fasting as unto God and not to impress people. They embrace a beautiful orthodoxy and a bold orthopraxy. They produce the fruit of the Spirit wherever they go: love, joy, peace, patience, kindness, goodness, faithfulness, gentleness, and self-control (Gal 5:22–23). As Jesus said, "By their fruit you will recognize them" (Matt 7:20).

Upper Room Reflection

Identify the major influences shaping your desires.

What does it mean to pray in Jesus' name?

How do you negotiate the tension between Jesus' "whatever-you-wish" promise and our wish-dreams?

How does the world see your good works and glorify your Father in heaven?

DAY 28

Relax

"As the Father has loved me, so have I loved you.
Now remain in my love. If you keep my commands,
you will remain in my love, just as I have kept my
Father's commands and remain in his love."

John 15:9–10

JESUS NEVER GOES SOLO. He is always singing the praises of the Father, reveling in his love, obedient to his will, and dependent on his power. If anyone could claim independence Jesus could. "For in him all things were created: things in heaven and on earth, visible and invisible, whether thrones or powers or rulers or authorities; all things have been created through him and for him. He is before all things, and in him all things hold together" (Col 1:16–17). But Jesus is the antithesis to the autonomous individual self. His work is always in concert with the Father and celebrated by the Spirit.

His communion with us issues out of his relationship with the Father and is affirmed by the Spirit. Most of us struggle with selfish autonomy, constantly thinking about ourselves. We're always wrestling with one thing or another, our vanity one day, our insecurity the next. Instead of resting in the family of God, we strive to make a name for ourselves or satisfy some urge. We vacillate between woe-is-me discouragement and one-upmanship pride. We flip-flop between a quest for success and a fight for survival. In opposition to all of this striving the God of comfort comes to us and invites us to remain in him. "Make your home with me," Jesus insists.

Jesus is not pining away to be our friend. We cannot project our relational needs on him. He is not longing to use us to fill his personal need. Father, Son, and Holy Spirit are never alone but always together as one. For God is never the solitary being that we can be, nor is God ever lonely. The autonomous individual self knows no parallel in the character of God. There never was a time when God was alone. His desire to make his home with us is motivated entirely out of self-sacrificing love and never out of pride of possession or a desire to control us. Jesus says, "Here I am! I stand at the door and knock. If anyone hears my voice and opens the door, I will come in and eat with that person, and they with me" (Rev 3:20). God's love is always a humble love. He waits for the invitation to come in, but we must never misconstrue his humble love for a tolerant permissiveness that puts up with our selfishness and sinfulness for the sake of relationship. Jesus prefaces his "I stand at the door and knock" invitation with these words: "Those whom I love I rebuke and discipline. So be earnest and repent" (Rev 3:19).

My six-year-old grandson Liam abides in his father's love for him. He is nurtured, fed, clothed, cared for, counseled, protected, and inspired daily in a loving family that he did not create nor control. Jesus used the father and son analogy to help his disciples grasp the meaning and fullness of his love for them. "As the Father has loved me" sets the precedent for all the love to follow: Jesus' love for us and our love for one another. Our first explicit indicator of what this love entails is the shocking truth that the Father loves the Son by giving him away on our behalf. This is a self-sacrificing, life-giving love. "For God so loved the world that he gave his one and only Son . . ." (John 3:16). The second indicator of the Father's love is that he "has placed everything in his hands" (John 3:35). Paradoxically, the Father gives the Son away and gives him authority over everything. The third indicator of the Father's love is that he grants life itself to the Son. To know the Son is to know the Father, and the Son does just what the Father tells him to do (John 5:26, 30). The Son's love is always a reflection of the Father's self-sacrificing, truth-keeping, life-giving love. We are invited to remain in Jesus' love in much the same way that my grandson is expected to remain in my son's love. The "asking," "telling," "show-ing," and "expecting," is all part of the daily discourse, the life to-gether, that shapes the soul, builds character, nurtures hope, and commands obedience.

The conditional nature of loving obedience and obedient love is more promise than threat. Bruner's translation helps here: "Just as much as the Father loved me—there! that is how much I have loved you. Make your home in this special love of mine (and relax)."[1] Jesus encourages rather than scolds. He reassures rather than rebukes. Covenant love transcends contractual obligation. Grace lifts the believer above the law, not to ignore or violate the law, but to fulfill the law of Christ. "If you keep my commands," re-move whatever mystery and confusion surrounds the call to love. What it means to remain in Jesus' love is not left to a flight of fancy or the spirit of the times. Love is not determined by our feelings, but by the commands of God. Command-keeping love is inspired by the one who "learned obedience from what he suffered and, once made perfect, he became the source of eternal salvation for all who obey him . . ." (Heb 5:8–9).

The tension between love and obedience is pulled taut even though the world wants love apart from the commands of God. Recently, a friend of mine sought my advice on a difficult matter. A gay couple is attending the church where my friend is the pastor. Both partners seem to be sincere seekers. They ask good questions about Christ and the church. Their involvement in the congrega-tion is sincere.

They have adopted a baby and they want their child to be included in the upcoming baby dedication. The temptation is to feel that the loving thing to do would be to dedicate the child even though the parents are violating the vowed commitment they will be asked to give: "Do you promise, in reliance upon the Holy Spirit and with the help of the Christian community, to do all in your

1. Bruner, *John*, 887.

power to guide your children in the Christian Faith and to lead them by your example into the life of Christian discipleship?" If the gay couple persists in asking good questions they are bound to wrestle with the church's biblical understanding of marriage and sexuality. As awkward as it may seem, I don't see how the church can remain faithful to God's word and recognize their marriage and dedicate the child. The whole church community is at stake, not just the feelings of the gay couple. Such a stand is difficult for all concerned, but necessary if the church is to practice obedient love. The cultural shift on gay marriage has been dramatic and will not likely be reversed. In the eyes of the world our failure to sanction and bless what the world celebrates will increasingly be seen as *morally* wrong and unloving. But if we fail to tether love to obedience we will soon find ourselves deeply confused and morally lost. The challenge before us is to remain in Jesus' love by obeying the Father's will. It is not always easy to place our trust in the Father's commands and relax, especially when the world is going in one direction and the path of discipleship is going in another. We have to be loving, but obedient love is never soft.

Upper Room Reflection

How does Jesus expect his relationship with the Father to parallel our relationship with him?

In a threatening world, how can you rest in Jesus' love?

How do you read the tone of Jesus' spiritual direction?

Describe your experience of the tension between love and obedience.

DAY 29

My Joy

*"I have told you this so that my joy may be in you
and that your joy may be complete."*

John 15:11

THE GOD WHO COMFORTS makes three promises—gives three gifts: 1) *"My peace* I give you. I do not give to you as the world gives" (John 14:27). 2) "If you keep my commands, you will remain in *my love* . . ." (John 15:10). 3) "I have told you this so that *my joy* may be in you and your joy may be complete" (John 15:11). Peace, love, and joy, are the benefits of discipleship, but not just any peace, love, and joy. This little possessive pronoun "my" makes all the difference. Peace with God and the peace of God can only come from the one who loved us enough to lay down his life for us. "This is love," wrote John, "not that we loved God, but that he loved us and sent his Son as an atoning sacrifice for our sins" (1 John 4:10). Only this real peace and sacrificial love is powerful enough to produce the complete joy promised by Jesus. Jesus' love for us is grounded in his obedience to the Father and our love for one another is grounded in our obedience to him and his commands.

Command-keeping love is not joyless drudgery, but the true secret to human flourishing and fulfillment. I learned early in life that obedience to my earthly father's will was in my best interest. His "commands" were not onerous; they made sense. He expected obedience from my brother and me, not for the sake of his authority and parental control, but for our well-being and moral character. Such was my father's selflessness that my brother and I naturally sought to please him. Our obedience was driven out of love, not fear. When I broke my father's clear "commands," like the time I swore at my mother, it seemed my father could move heaven and earth to make his point. I knew that love and respect were not optional and disobedience would not be tolerated. In the "ordered universe" of our home, I knew the joy of loving obedience and obedient love. True joy is the opposite of self-indulgence and willful pleasure. It is the deep sense of harmony and security that comes from being at peace with God and making our home with Jesus. Jesus gives us the peace, love, and righteousness that makes joy possible.

Jesus' conversation from the upper room to Gethsemane underscores the purpose of Christian communication. We have a responsibility to nurture and be nurtured by the Word of God. It should be our passion as it was Jesus' passion to convey the truth about joy. "I have told you this," Jesus said, "so that my joy may be in you and that your joy may be complete." Parents and pastors ought to share a similar passion to convey the truth about joy. Friends, too, should speak up so that Jesus' joy is shared among their friends. God is pleased when the conversation leads to real joy. We don't need a sanctuary or a pulpit to convey this truth. Our companions along the way will be frail human beings, struggling with grief and loss (John 16:6), but let the theme be joy—"my joy in you."

We cannot engineer our own happiness even though we try so hard. We are like the patient who is waiting desperately for a new kidney and an organ donor comes along and says in effect, "my kidney in you." We can grasp the concreteness of this specific gift, its selfless sacrifice and its life-giving health. A friend of ours gave his kidney to his niece. I can assure you that there is nothing abstract about the deep bond of gratitude and love between them. I wish we could grasp Christ's joy in this way. Only the transplant of Jesus' joy into us can complete our joy.

Jesus' Sermon on the Mount Beatitudes serve as a spiritual diagnostic indicating the state of grace that makes us good organ recipients. "My joy in you," or as the Beatitudes say, "Deep happiness," belongs to those who acknowledge their desperate need for God and their inability to merit salvation. *Each one of the Beatitudes is a description of grace-shaped receptivity to the will of God.* These eight fundamental emotional attitudes, eight convictions of the soul, eight character qualities of the inner person describe the true recipients of Jesus' transplantable joy. We are poor and in need of God's riches. We are sin-sick and in need of God's forgiveness. We are weak and resting in God's strength. We are hungry and dependent upon God's provision. We are merciful because of God's mercy. We are holy because of God's holy love. We are peacemakers because of God's peace. True joy is as far removed from the self-made man or woman as you can imagine. We could never have created this joy. No, not in a thousand years. This joy—"my joy"—belongs to us only because it belongs to Jesus.

Upper Room Reflection

How do Jesus' gifts correspond to your deepest desires and longings?

When you hear the word *obedience*, what comes to mind?

What does Jesus' transplantable joy mean to you?

Compare the world's path to joy and Jesus' path to joy.

DAY 30

No Greater Love

"My command is this: Love each other as I have loved you. Greater love has no one than this: to lay down one's life for one's friends. You are my friends if you do what I command. I no longer call you servants, because a servant does not know his master's business. Instead, I have called you friends, for everything that I learned from my Father I have made known to you."

John 15:12–15

JESUS KEPT NOTHING BACK from his friends. He shared everything with them. "For everything that I learned from my Father I have made known to you" is the bottom line of costly discipleship (John 15:15). Full disclosure is the prerequisite for fully devoted followers of Jesus. There is no better expression of true friendship than to share with your friend everything God has given to you.

To love others in the same way that we have been loved by Jesus turns the world upside down. Beatitude-based receptivity to the peace, love, and joy of Christ is bound to have salt-and-light impact. "My joy in you" opens up before us never imagined demonstrations of love that transcend the typical cultures of shame and honor, law and guilt, low esteem and high esteem. Christians no longer play by the cultural rules that govern human interaction and determine winners and losers. They transcend the usual rules of the game because they follow the Master. Jesus called for "unusual Christians in all the usual situations."[1]

Malcolm Gladwell in *David and Goliath* explores the ability of "outsiders" to turn difficult situations to their advantage. Underdogs and misfits find a way to beat the system and rise above their disadvantages. They are risk-takers and rule-benders. They do what it takes to get ahead. They compensate for their weaknesses by being borderline disagreeable and pragmatically deceptive. They may bluff and bully, but they don't surrender easily to failure. Instead of adapting to the world, they find ways to make the world adapt to them. Gladwell offers a compelling description of the underdog getting the job done by hook or by crook. His perspective reminds me of the shrewd manager in Jesus' parable. The manager was accused of wasting his master's funds so he cleverly made some quick deals with his master's debtors. By slicing their debts in half he made a few fast friends. When the master heard about it, he was impressed. He commended the dishonest manager because he acted shrewdly. Then Jesus made this telling observation: "For the people of this world are more shrewd in dealing with their own kind than are the people of the light" (Luke 16:8). What underdogs do out of self-love to get ahead, Christ's followers ought to do out of Christ's love for the sake of others. This is the greater love.

New commandment obedience reaffirms what Jesus has been saying in his upper room discourse and captures his conversation along the way. There is no escaping the call to obedience; to believe is to obey and to obey is to believe. Salt-and-light impact and true heart righteousness produces visible, social righteousness. The guiding principle for visible righteousness is life-affirming: "Let your light shine before people, that they may see your good deeds and praise your Father in heaven" (Matt 5:16). The command to love is "not a strange spiritual gymnastic; it is as human as it can be."[2] But it runs contrary to our sinful human nature and strikes us as exceedingly difficult. We do not come by this love

1. Bruner, *Matthew*, vol. 1, 260.
2. Bruner, *John*, 890.

automatically and we cannot ignore its impossibility apart from the grace of God. It takes a lot of prayerful practice before this love even begins to feel natural. Humanly speaking, we are wired to play the cultural game in our low-esteem/high-esteem culture. We naturally leverage everything to our advantage in order to gain the upper hand. But as we have seen the Jesus way is radically different. The principle of the world is "your life for mine." The principle of the cross is "my life for yours." Yes, we want to be loved as only Jesus can love us but it is also true that we must love as Jesus would love. This is why Paul prayed, may love "abound more and more in knowledge and depth of insight, so that you may be able to discern what is best and may be pure and blameless for the day of Christ, filled with the fruit of righteousness that comes through Jesus Christ—to the glory and praise of God" (Phil 1:9–11).

The "greater works" (14:12) and the "greater love" are two ways of describing the same phenomenon. What makes the greater works great is the greater love of the crucified, risen, and ascended Christ. We have received this love not only for ourselves but for the sake of others. We have gone beyond servants and slaves; we are now friends and partners in the mission of God. "Jesus is not only our Friend, but our Commanding Officer. . . . We disciples are not only his family; we are his troops. . . .The surprise now is that the troops can actually become the close friends of this Commanding Officer when they keep his heart orders."[3]

Upper Room Reflection

What does it mean to have a friend in Jesus?

How can we love others the way we have been loved by Jesus?

Is the principle of the cross realistic in a pragmatic world?

How can Jesus be both our Friend and our Commanding Officer?

3. Ibid., 891.

DAY 31

Chosen

*"You did not choose me, but I chose you and ap-
pointed you so that you might go and bear fruit—
fruit that will last—and so that whatever you ask
in my name the Father will give you. This is my
command: Love one another."*

John 15:16–17

WHEN IT COMES TO friendship and marriage, to be chosen by
the other—our friend or our beloved—means more to us than
our freedom to choose. We take such pride in being free agents,
but in our deepest relationships we want to know that someone
else, someone special has taken the initiative and has chosen us.
Children, whether adopted or conceived, rest in the love that they
are chosen by their parents. Love shapes their world long before
they can begin to grasp the meaning of being chosen. There is no
room in healthy relationships for the imperial self. All the best
emotions belong to those who humbly, gratefully acknowledge that
the power of choice is trumped by the power of love. We rest in our
chosen-ness. Relational love is not a performance-driven human
achievement but a slow work of God's grace. C. S. Lewis writes: "A
secret Master of Ceremonies has been at work. Christ, who said to
the disciples, 'You have not chosen me, but I have chosen you,' can
truly say to every group of Christian friends, 'You have not chosen
one another but I have chosen you for one another.' The Friendship
is not a reward for our discrimination and good taste in finding

one another out. It is the instrument by which God reveals to each the beauties of all the others."[1]

The story behind our relational life is similar to the truth behind our salvation. Divine providence is the blessing of God's great faithfulness going before us, conducting the symphony, weaving the tapestry, supervising the project, writing the poetry that we call life. We can rest secure in our friendship with God and in the wisdom he has shared with us. We're not one decision away from blowing it. The fruitfulness of our lives does not depend on our feeble choices. We are not victims of blind fate. Jesus reminds us, yet again, that we rest in his abiding presence. He is the vine, not the branch. The Father is the gardener. We have not chosen this path of discipleship to turn it into our own spiritual quest and moral crusade. "The initiative is wholly his. We have only to 'abide' in the vine. Therein lies the source of the godly confidence and even the boldness of the disciple."[2]

We have been chosen and appointed ("set aside") for a purpose. The same Greek verb used here for "set aside" was used by Jesus for himself when he said, "Greater love has no one than this: to lay down ('set aside') one's life for one's friends" (John 15:13). Like our Lord, we are called to take up our cross and follow him. The option is not available to us to choose between being chosen and commissioned. We cannot choose Jesus as our Savior and then decline the commander's commission. The call to salvation includes the call to service, sacrifice, and simplicity. Jesus is both Savior and Lord, or he is nothing at all. He is our friend and commander. We have been chosen for a purpose and the purpose is to bear fruit that lasts. Faithfulness and fruitfulness are inseparable. We have been saved to serve.

Disciples are called to "set aside" or "lay down" their lives for the sake of others. The command to one another must never be reduced to group-selfishness. In our earlier reflection on John 13:34 we drew on Søren Kierkegaard's insight that the world rightly condemns

1. Lewis, *The Four Loves*, 89.
2. Newbigin, *The Light Has Come*, 204.

me-only self-love as selfish, but when selfishness forms a group of other selfish people the world calls it love. The world demands that selfish people give up a measure of selfishness in order to enjoy the privileges of group-selfishness. This kind of self-love sacrifices God's love and "locks God out or at most takes him along for the sake of appearance."[3] Worldly self-love comes in many forms: ethnic compatibility, tribal affinity, denominational loyalty, social familiarity, and generational identity. But to love as Christ loves is to know the difference between "group-selfishness" and being the neighbor Christ calls us to be. Disciples who "become a comfortable, exclusivistic huddle" are no longer in the vine.[4] They are nothing more than withered, dead branches, good for nothing but the fire.

Once again Jesus repeats his extravagant promise. Only this time, instead of saying "I will do whatever you ask in my name, so that the Father may be glorified in the Son," he says, "Whatever you ask in my name the Father will give you" (John 14:13; 15:16). The variation only serves to underscore the essential oneness between the Father and the Son. Prayerful dependence on God for the sake of the mission of God is the key to producing lasting fruit. We are chosen, set aside, informed, and empowered to bear fruit. We are at home with Jesus in much the same way that a child is at home in a loving family.

Upper Room Reflection

Why do we prefer to be chosen than to choose?

Where does the power and wisdom to love others come from?

Why is it easy to confuse group-selfishness with love?

What does lasting fruit look like to you?

3. Kierkegaard, *Works of Love*, 123.
4. Carson, *The Gospel According to John*, 523.

Hate Defined

"If the world hates you, keep in mind that it hated me first. If you belonged to the world, it would love you as its own. As it is, you do not belong to the world, but I have chosen you out of the world. That is why the world hates you."

John 15:18–19

JESUS' CONVERSATION ON THE way takes a decisive turn. Until now the spiritual direction has been reassuring and empowering. It has been about making our home with Jesus. The disciples are reminded that they are chosen, appointed, loved, and befriended. As we put ourselves in their shoes we are encouraged by what Jesus has to say. We are in the vine where we belong, pruned by the Father gardener so we will bear lasting fruit. But on their walk from the upper room to Gethsemane Jesus turns a street corner and shifts the topic from being loved to being hated.

The God who comforts covers a subject that most comforters avoid—hate. *Hate* is a strong word suggesting a vehement and vindictive spirit. It is vividly portrayed in the contorted face of rage and in the guttural voice of anger, but it also can be expressed in subtle and covert ways. Hate is a four-letter word encompassing malice, contempt, resentment, bitterness, spite, and blame. It can be blatant or hidden, but hate is painfully real. To hate is to detest, loath, abhor, ridicule, and condemn. Hate in the abstract is bad enough, but to be hated in person triggers an adrenaline rush that causes our heart rate to quicken. We tend to avoid the word *hate*. It sounds too extreme. We don't like using the word, but Jesus used it to describe the world's reaction to his followers.

Jesus used the word as a verb in a conditional clause: "If the world hates you . . ." We may like that little word *if* because it implies (or so we think) that Jesus' reference to hate may not apply to us. We can skip this concern because it applies to first-century persecution or to today's persecution hot spots like Sudan, Syria, and North Korea. Our part of the world doesn't really hate Christians. People like us and if they don't, they at least tolerate our Christian ways. But we should not dismiss Jesus' warning about hate too quickly. We are like naive swimmers on a beautiful summer day who ignore the ocean lifeguard's repeated warning of rip currents. Appearances belie the danger below the surface. Jesus' conditional clause leaves little doubt as to the world's reaction to Christ's followers. It's not so much "If the world hates you," as "When the world hates you."

Jesus gave three reasons why the world hates his disciples and each reason relates to believers everywhere (John 15:18–16:4). First, the world hates believers because they don't belong to the world. Jesus has chosen them out of the world. Second, believers are hated because of the exclusive truth claim of Christ. The world is not willing to accept that Jesus was sent by the Father and is one with God. Third, the world hates believers because of the convicting power of the gospel of grace. The gospel provokes rejection and rebellion. On the basis of these three reasons the grounds for hate are fundamentally theological even though the surface reason for the world's reaction may have to do with sexual practices or lifestyle convictions.

If what Jesus says about the world hating his disciples is irrelevant to us there is always the possibility that it is because we belong too much to the world. If we are in the world and of the world, then we are just like the world. And we all know that the world does not hate itself. In the absence of the world's animosity we can assume we have become innocuous, lukewarm Christians. The Danish Christian thinker Søren Kierkegaard believed that there was nothing in the popular Christianity of his day that warranted the world's persecution. Christians were so completely assimilated into the culture that there was no real difference between a Christian and a non-Christian. Christians shared the world's passions for the good life. Everyone was a Christian, because no one was a Christian. The world does not hate the world, Kierkegaard observed, when it discovers itself in Christianity. Christians cannot be at home in the world and at the same be "a stranger and a pilgrim in the world."[1]

If we are like the world in almost every respect except for a few private religious ideas we can expect to gain the world's approval. But if we become like Jesus as he is presented in the Bible through the fellowship of his sufferings and the power of his resurrection, we should be prepared for the world's rejection. The way to know Christ is to become like Jesus and thus his life transforms every aspect of our lives. His spirituality is our model for true worship. His teaching is the ground for our ethical actions; his self-understanding is the pattern for our self-awareness; his self-sacrifice is the paradigm for our service; his bodily resurrection is the hope of our resurrection. His method of evangelism is the strategy for our witness and his call for justice and righteousness is our mission. Make no mistake: this Christ-centered life will provoke the world's anger. Dale Bruner observes that there is a realism about the last half of John 15's world speech that balances the joy of the first half of John 15's home speech in a sobering way. To be at home with Jesus is to be at odds with the world. Jesus is bracing his disciples for this less pleasant reality in becoming Christians. It would not have been fair for Jesus to send his disciples out with only his home (and love) teaching without also giving them his world (and "hate-from-the-world" teaching) in order fully to equip them for their task in the real world.[2]

1. Kierkegaard, *Attack Upon "Christendom,"* 42.

2. Bruner, *John,* 903.

Upper Room Reflection

If you had been with Jesus what would you have thought about his focus on persecution and hate?

How can Jesus' realism encourage his disciples today?

Why is a tolerant world intolerant of Christians?

Discuss: If we are hated, let it be for all the right reasons.

DAY 33

Persecution

"Remember what I told you: 'A servant is not greater than his master.' If they persecuted me, they will persecute you also. If they obeyed my teaching, they will obey yours also. They will treat you this way because of my name, for they do not know the one who sent me."

John 15:20–21

JESUS IS THE PRECEDENT-SETTING reason for the world's hate. "If the world hates you, keep in mind that it hated me first" (John 15:18). He is our master and we are his disciples. "A servant is not greater than his master." We share in his path to the cross. His narrative becomes our narrative. We lean in to his cruciform strategy of submission and sacrifice. But if the world hates us for any other reason than for a cause that can be traced back to Jesus we have a serious problem. If we are self-righteous instead of heart righteous; if we are all doom and gloom, instead of salt and light, then we are to blame and our offense before the world is of our own making. If we show hate instead of love or infidelity instead of fidelity, the world has every reason to charge us with hypocrisy.

Too many Christians feel it is their duty to fight fire with fire. They play the world's high-stakes poker game, saying in effect, "I'll match your hate and raise the ante." They are threatened by the "secular" culture and feel compelled to vent their anger against the world. Their resentment and fear run deep. Their vitriolic rhetoric and slander against their opponents is not an indication of strength and boldness, but of fear and hate. Frustrated Christians feel that their culture is slipping away from them in spite of their best efforts to "change the world for Christ." We need a fresh reminder that the Christian before the world is like Jesus before Pilate. We need to hear Jesus' words over and over again to stay on mission: "My kingdom is not of this world. If it were, my servants would fight to prevent my arrest by the Jewish leaders. But now my kingdom is from another place" (John 18:36). Christ's followers should be known by their love, not their hate, but the sad fact is that many Christians have learned much more from the world than they have from Jesus.

Since Jesus was hated for all the right reasons, disciples in twenty-first-century New York or Hong Kong can hope to be hated for all the right reasons, too. I suppose that Judah was more like America than modern-day Sudan or North Korea. Righteousness and justice were ostensibly honored in Judah by the religious and political authorities. Temple religion vied with civil religion to preserve the moral order and spiritual authority. Nevertheless the "good" forces of culture came together to take down Jesus. They did so because Jesus' good news and good works belonged to a whole new order of being. Jesus inaugurated a kingdom ethic, a new way of life consistent with the absolute reign of God (absolute in the sense of being absolved of all cultural contingencies). Therefore anyone who follows Jesus loses everything to gain Christ (Phil 3:8–10). A narrow view of religious life with its safe compartmentalizing of the sacred and secular is thrown away. Middle-class values and comfortable ideologies of the left or right need to be cast off.

It is scandalous that one who healed the sick, loved the outcast, and transformed the sinner should die a hideously cruel death by Roman crucifixion. Surely this radical paradox crossed the mind of Jesus as they navigated the streets of Jerusalem on their way to Gethsemane. What kind of world do we live in that sentences holy and compassionate men and women to die? Jesus exposes the fact that the political and religious authorities in the world system are not on the side of righteousness. Greed, pride, and hate control the power elite. Jesus became a victim for the sake of righteousness. It was impossible for anyone living in the first century to gloss over the practical social consequences of following Jesus. The cross made sure of that. Early Christians knew that their lives were marked by the cross, but many contemporary Christians give the impression that a decision for Jesus simply involves submitting mentally to the idea that Jesus died for our sins.

Jesus is the precedent-setting standard for both persecution and proclamation. The gospel preached, witnessed, and lived in the tradition of Jesus will incite opposition and inspire obedience. Many in the world will hate Jesus' disciples just as they hated Jesus. "If they persecuted me, they will persecute you also" (John 15:20). But some in the world will embrace the good news proclaimed by Jesus, "for God so loved the world" (John 3:16), and they will be transformed by the gospel. "If they obeyed my teaching, they will obey yours also" (John 15:20).

Jesus makes it clear that the one being rejected is God himself. The world may excuse its rejection by blaming the institutional church or greedy pastors or religious hypocrites, but in the end, all these real sins will not stand as a valid excuse against the word of God and the testimony of Jesus. But the world is not the big issue here. The big question is this: Are we willing to follow Jesus and take up our cross and follow him?

Upper Room Reflection

Should Christians vent their resentment against the world?

How does Jesus' interaction with Pilate serve as an example for the believer's interaction with the world?

In your experience how has the gospel incited opposition and inspired obedience?

How does Jesus' spiritual direction compare to what you have been taught in church?

Guilt-Driven Hate

"If I had not come and spoken to them, they would
not be guilty of sin; but now they have no excuse for
their sin. Whoever hates me hates my Father as well."

John 15:22–23

THE POWER OF THE gospel moves people to repentance and forgiveness or rejection and rebellion. Either we turn to God for salvation or we turn away from God for judgment. Jesus is "the true light that gives light to everyone coming into the world. . . . He came to that which was his own, but his own did not receive not receive him. Yet to all who did receive him, to those who believed in his name, he gave the right to become children of God" (John 1:9,11–12). The gospel of Jesus divides humanity between guilt and grace: "This is the verdict: Light has come into the world, but people loved darkness instead of light because their deeds were evil. Everyone who does evil hates the light, and will not come into the light for fear their deeds will be exposed. But whoever lives by the truth comes into the light, so that it may be seen plainly that what they have done has been done in the sight of God" (John 3:19–21).

Jesus' gospel preaching did what the law did *only better*! Everyone is guilty of breaking the law. We all stand condemned before the holy God. The law of God was given "so that every mouth may be silenced and the whole world held accountable to God. . . . Through the law we become conscious of our sin" (Rom 3:19–20). However the convicting power of the law was lost to those who used the law to justify themselves. They assumed that trying to keep "the written code" was sufficient for salvation. "You, then, who teach others, do you teach yourself?" (Rom 2:21).

But now the written law of God, handed down through the centuries, is eclipsed by God incarnate—God came *in person*. "The Word became flesh and made his dwelling among us. We have seen his glory, the glory of the one and only Son, who came from the Father, full of grace and truth. . . . No one has ever seen God, but the one and only Son, who is himself God and is in the closest relationship with the Father, has made him known" (John 1:14, 18). "Jesus is the one who 'narrates' God on the plane of human existence."[1] The law and the whole sacrificial system did two things: it proved we are sinners and it pictured our need for the mercy of God. But now that Jesus has come preaching the good news we have no excuse for claiming we're "good enough." We have no excuse for shunning his gracious offer of salvation through his atoning sacrifice for our sins.

Just as people twisted the law of God to suit their own self-serving, self-justifying ways, we face the danger of watering down the gospel and to make it all about self-esteem. A feel-good-about-yourself gospel is no substitute for the gospel of grace that leads to true repentance and deep dependence on the mercy of God. Christ-less Christianity robs the gospel of its convicting power. We want to placate the wounded hearts of lost, self-centered, fun-loving narcissists, forgetting that Paul said, "For the message of the cross is foolishness to those who are perishing, but to us who are being saved it is the power of God" (1 Cor 1:18). The prophet Isaiah described the Suffering Servant—Jesus—as one who "had no beauty or majesty to attract us to him, nothing in his appearance that we should desire him" (Isa 53:2). The gospel of grace comes off looking like the beat-up Jesus when it is delivered to people who resist the convicting power of the gospel of grace. When Jesus says, "Whoever hates me hates my Father as well," we ought to recall the vivid images of Isaiah 53. To put it simply, Jesus warned

1. Carson, *John*, 527.

us ahead of time that those who deliver the gospel will be despised and rejected like their Lord.

Jesus braces his disciples for the guilt-driven backlash of a world antagonized by the gospel of grace. All who follow the path of the Suffering Servant can expect to be oppressed and afflicted in the same way that Jesus was. Martin Luther marveled at how God's wonderful plan for church growth defied human understanding. Luther insisted that Jesus' conversation on the way to Gethsemane drove "out of the hearts of the disciples the erroneous delusion" that the gospel will meet with worldly success. Instead of "worldly and temporal good and honor and power and peace," Christ's ambassadors will "suffer shame and death."[2] He concluded, "Those who know Christ—the true Christians—will accept Christ's classification and be numbered with the minority, who have the Word and the knowledge of Christ, and they will suffer persecution for the faith rather than, for the sake of friendship and honor of this world, to belong to those who, condemned by Christ, are the bitterest foes of God and of the Church, and who cannot see the kingdom of God, nor be saved."[3]

Upper Room Reflection

Do you agree that the gospel leads either to repentance or rebellion?

How did you first hear about the gospel of God's grace?

What are the dangers of twisting the gospel into something the world wants?

How does Jesus prepare us for the world's reaction to gospel?

2. Luther, *The Complete Sermons*, vol. 2, 262.
3. Ibid., 270.

DAY 35

Senseless Hate

*"If I had not done among them the works no one else
did, they would not be guilty of sin. As it is they have
seen, and yet they have hated both me and my Father.
But this is to fulfill what is written in their Law: 'They
hated me without reason.'"*

John 15:24–25

JESUS USES STRONG LANGUAGE to describe unbelief. The thought
expressed here parallels the preceding verses. "If I had not come
and spoken. . . . If I had not done among them the works . . . they
would not be guilty of sin." But God in the flesh came, speaking
the truth of God and performing the works of God, and the world
refused to believe. His witness and his works testify against unbelief. "They have no excuse for their sin" (John 15:22). Jesus sees the
world's unbelief for what it is—hate. "Whoever hates me hates my
Father as well. . . .They have hated both me and my Father" (John
15:23). Synonymous parallelism in Hebrew poetry is for emphasis
and Jesus uses that same literary technique to critique the world's
rejection. The world has no excuse for its sin and the world has no
excuse for its hate.

Jesus takes this hate personally. "Whoever hates me . . ." Unbelief is not a difference of opinion or a doctrinal dispute or a clash
of perspectives. Jesus sees unbelief as an in your face personal rejection of God's love and mercy. It is shocking to hear Jesus frame
unbelief in this way. We tend to placate and pacify unbelievers for

fear of offending them. We are not bold when it comes to the laying out the consequences of unbelief. We want to say that God's love overrides human rejection and unbelief. But Jesus is not having any of it. He distills unbelief down to hate.

Jesus shows little regard here for the dilemma of unbelief. He offers no patience for the person struggling with doubt or wrestling with belief. His assessment of unbelief is unapologetic. Jesus takes away the middle ground between unbelief and angry atheism. He assesses the unbeliever as an enemy of God. The little old man or woman with a sweet disposition yet who wilfully dismisses the gospel as unnecessary is described by Jesus as a God-hater—an antichrist. "Who is the liar?" John asks in his epistle. "It is whoever denies that Jesus is the Christ. Such a person is the antichrist—denying the Father and the Son. No one who denies the Son has the Father; whoever acknowledges the Son has the Father also" (1 John 2:22–23). All the variations of unbelief that we rationalize and excuse are swept away by Jesus as he heads to the cross.

The disciples would later recall this conversation and realize that Jesus was preparing them for the world's harsh rejection. The God who comforts forewarns Christ's followers that they will be on the receiving end of hostility in the form of abuse, slander, ridicule, accusation, and discrimination. The opposition may not take the form of state-sponsored persecution or legal retribution or imprisonment, but the backlash is real. Another reason for Jesus' "hate from the world" spiritual direction may have been to encourage believers not to blame themselves for the world's rejection. If unbelievers failed to respond to Jesus' witness and works, they will fail to respond to our proclamation of the gospel. There is no excuse for their rejection and no guilt on the part of the disciple. Finally, it is a reminder to love our enemies, to return love for hate, to seek reconciliation instead of retaliation, and to pray for our enemies. Hate is never an excuse for believers to fight the world with the weapons of the world. Love instead of hate is demonstrated in full in the hours leading to the cross.

By quoting a line from the Psalms, "They hated me without reason," Jesus leads the disciples in a prayerful response to hate.

The place to go in the heat of opposition is to the Lord in prayer. When the world's rejection is especially painful and the reason for the hate passes all understanding the Christian prays. A prayed-out lament is different from a vindictive venting! Psalms 35 and 69 instruct us in how to bring the world's painful rejection to the Lord. Through prayer we are reminded of God's great love and his sure salvation. We cry out, "Rescue me from the mire, do not let me sink; deliver me from those who hate me, from the deep waters" (Ps 69:13–14).

Upper Room Reflection

How do you respond to Jesus' description of the world's reaction to the gospel?

Why isn't Jesus more sympathetic to unbelievers?

How is Jesus' description of the world's hate comforting?

How can believers learn to give a Jesus-like response to hate?

DAY 36

The Spirit of Truth

*"When the Advocate comes, whom I will send to you
from the Father—the Spirit of truth who goes out from
the Father—he will testify about me. And you also must
testify, for you have been with me from the beginning."*

John 15:26–27

THE GOINGS AND COMINGS of Jesus stay in the forefront of his conversation with his disciples. He will leave them soon—physically. He will die on the cross and leave them for a short while and then following the resurrection and his appearances he will ascend to the Father. In lieu of his physical absence he comes to all of his disciples in the comforting fourfold promise of his future coming, the Parousia ("I will come back and take you to be with me that you also may be where I am" [John 14:3]); and in the coming of the Spirit of truth, the Paraclete ("And I will ask the Father, and he will give you another advocate to help you and be with you forever—the Spirit of truth" [John 14:16–17]); and in the coming of the resurrection, the Passion ("Before long, the world will not see me anymore, but you will see me. Because I live, you also will live" [John 14:19]); and finally in the coming of his abiding spiritual Presence ("If you remain in me and I in you, you will bear much fruit" [John 15:5]).

If we look to the world for affirmation and moral support we will be deeply disappointed and disillusioned. The believer who expects to be congratulated by the world for sharing the gospel and

127

practicing the Jesus way will soon realize that the world hates Jesus and his followers. This hatred may be subtle and covert but nevertheless real even in a Christendom culture. This is why we need the coordinated support of the Father, Son, and Holy Spirit. We are not alone. The Father and the Son team up to send the Spirit and the sending of the Spirit is much like the sending of the Son.[1] In the absence of Jesus' physical presence we have the pervasive, powerful, and personal presence of the Paraclete ("the one who is called alongside"). Imagine the finest lawyer you have ever met combined with the wisest counselor, the most encouraging friend, and the best teacher, and you have a faint inkling of the gift of the Holy Spirit to you personally and to the church. Because of the advocacy and empowerment of the Spirit we have the promise of "greater works" and the wisdom of Christ.

"When the Advocate comes . . . *he will testify about me.*" The focus of the Spirit's advocacy is Jesus Christ. Against the world's unbelief and hate the Spirit takes the lead in growing Christ's church, establishing the biblical canon, and proclaiming Christ to every people, tribe, language, and nation. The book of Acts records what Jesus *began* to do, and what he now *continues* to do through the Holy Spirit and the body of Christ. In Luke's two-volume Christ-book, the Gospel describes Jesus' earthly ministry and Acts describes the beginning of his heavenly ministry, which continues today in the Spirit and in life and ministry of the church.

On the streets of Jerusalem that night, Jesus prepared his original band of disciples to testify about him ("for you have been with me from the beginning"). The Holy Spirit takes the primary lead, but the witness of the apostles is also essential. The divine/human incarnational pattern remains in effect. The Spirit of truth and the body of Christ focus on the work and witness of Christ to fulfill the mission of God. The line of succession of apostolic authority is not handed down through a single apostle, but through the Spirit to all those who are in Christ.

1. Beasley-Murray, *John*, 276.

Jesus' conversation on the way to Gethsemane has two horizons in view: the original apostles and all the believers who through the centuries follow their Spirit-inspired witness. The historical Jesus said these words and the contemporary Jesus in the Spirit strengthens and comforts us as we read them.

The apostles were eager to include us in that "beginning." They were with Jesus from the beginning, but their testimony always takes us back to the beginning. "That which was from the beginning, which we have heard, which we have seen with out eyes, which we have looked at and our hands have touched—this we proclaim concerning the Word of Life" (1 John 1:1). In the Spirit, we establish our own beginning in Christ. "As for you," John wrote, "see that what you have heard from the beginning remains in you. If it does, you also will remain in the Son and in the Father. And this is what he promised us—eternal life" (1 John 2:24–25). And again, "For this is the message you heard from the beginning: We should love one another" (1 John 3:11). Faithfulness to the end proves true faith from the beginning.

The Spirit makes sure that Jesus' imperative, "You also must testify," is music to our ears. This is not an imposed duty but a reminder of our true love. The apostolic testimony is free of cliche and ambiguity—is ours? We have become so accustomed to the bland recital of religious rhetoric that our minds shift into neutral the moment we hear it. The New Testament Christ-explicitness is personal and penetrating. Nothing rote. The apostles insisted on using the name of Christ boldly and often, without jargon and empty god-talk.

Apart from the Holy Spirit we can do nothing, but in the Spirit we have the courage and the wisdom to bear witness to Jesus Christ, even when we are "hated without reason." The promised support of the whole Trinity is not made to a church successful in the eyes of the world. "It is made to the Church which shares the tribulation and humiliation of Jesus, the tribulation which arises from faithfulness to the truth in a world which is dominated by the lie."[2] Regardless of the world's reaction we have an Advocate who encourages and empowers our witness.

Upper Room Reflection

What comes to mind when you think of being comforted?

How does God's comfort counter our expectations for comfort?

How does Jesus' description of the Spirit of truth change your understanding of the Holy Spirit?

What do you say to the person who says, "I don't care about the truth. I just want to be happy"?

2. Newbigin, *The Light Has Come*, 208.

DAY 37

The Big Picture

"All this I have told you so that you will not fall away. They will put you out of the synagogue; in fact, the time is coming when anyone who kills you will think they are offering a service to God. They will do such things because they have not known the Father or me. I have told you this, so that when their time comes you will remember that I warned you about them. I did not tell you this from the beginning because I was with you, but now I am going to him who sent me. None of you asks me, 'Where are you going?' Rather you are filled with grief because I have said these things."

John 16:1–6

To be forewarned is to be prepared and *sobered*. The temptation is real to either fall away because of persecution or to drift away because of indifference (Heb 2:1). Coming just hours before his arrest, the timing of Jesus' conversation was crucial for the early disciples. His message remains critical for all disciples including later disciples like ourselves. Although Jesus told the disciples at least three times that he was going to die and rise again, he knew that they held to their cherished notions of a triumphant political Messiah who would overthrow Rome and reestablish David's kingdom. Earlier, he warned his disciples that they would face persecution, that they would be "flogged in the synagogues" and "hated by everyone because of me" (Matt 10:17,22), but in the immediacy of his departure he drove this depressing scenario home.

Up until now whatever persecution or slander the disciples experienced was buffered by Jesus. Jesus was always right there absorbing most of the rejection himself and proclaiming the good news of the kingdom. But after that night, the world's unbelief and hate would be taken out on the disciples directly. That was the tough news that Jesus shared with his disciples as he walked to Gethsemane. Jesus said, "Whoever hates me hates my Father," but now he adds another difficult truth: "Whoever hates me *hates you* and my Father as well." Even more tragic is the fact those who vent this hate are steeped in religion. They think "they are offering a service to God." Every religion, including Christendom religion, has hated Christ's followers. Jesus gives the verdict against Jews and Christians alike, "because they have not known the Father or me."

Canon Andrew White, the Vicar of St. George's Cathedral in Baghdad, is a contemporary voice calling attention to this ancient truth. In his 2013 book, *Father, Forgive*, he wrote: "The sad fact is, religion is very much tied up with violence. As Archbishop William Temple said during [World War II], 'When religion goes wrong, it goes very wrong.' The apostle John, recording the words of Jesus in his gospel wrote, 'the time is coming when anyone who kills you will think they are offering a service to God. They will do such things because they have not known the Father or me' (John 16:2–3). This is what we have witnessed in our time."[1]

New Testament theologian Don Carson writes: "Christians have often discovered that the most dangerous oppression comes not from careless pagans but from zealous adherents to religious faith, and from other ideologues. A sermon was preached when Cranmer was burned at the stake. Christians have faced severe persecution performed in the name of Yahweh, in the name of Allah, in the name of Marx—and in the name of Jesus."[2]

1. Quoted in George, "Silence and Solidarity."
2. Carson, *John*, 531.

The great paradox here is that the gospel of Christ that is designed to destroy the walls of hostility between God and humankind often provokes hostility. The old paganisms and the new messianisms fight against the church with everything they have. Newbigin writes: "Once the gospel is preached and there is a community which lives by the gospel, then the question of the ultimate meaning of history is posed and other messiahs appear. *So the crisis of history is deepened.* Even more significant as an example of this development than the rise of Marxism is the rise of Islam. Islam, which means simply submission, is the mightiest of all the post-Christian movements which claim to offer the kingdom of God without the cross. The denial of the crucifixion is and must always be central to Islamic teaching."[3]

Jesus is about to depart (on the cross) and he is deeply concerned that the disciples understand the fallout (excommunication and execution) so they do not fall away from the faith. "I have told you this, so that when their time comes you will remember that I warned you about them (the haters)" (John 16:4). His passion to strengthen and prepare his disciples that night was a brave act of self-denial and costly love that ought to inspire us to prepare young believers to weather the storms of hostility and hate. Many of our young disciples go off to university naive, without an informed understanding of the opposition they will face intellectually, socially, physically, emotionally, sexually, and spiritually. They face an exclusive humanism, a radical pluralism, and a dogmatic materialism that writes off even the possibility of faith in Christ. They take classes from professors who think that it is ridiculous to even discuss the subject of God and revelation. There is little debate between belief and unbelief, because belief in Jesus Christ is no longer considered possible or plausible. Universal truth is swept away with philosophical slight of hand. As my neighbor said, "You don't honestly believe in that stuff anymore do you?" Young disciples enter a world where universal truth has been categorically

3. Newbigin, *The Gospel in a Pluralist Society*, 122

ruled out. An immature, Sunday school-ish faith is soon crushed on the university campus.[4]

Jesus interrupts the flow of his own conversation with a sad observation: "None of you asks me, 'Where are you going?' Rather, you are filled with grief because I have said these things" (John 16:5–6). The pathos of that particular moment comes through in the failed comprehension of the disciples, who cannot grasp the big picture. Their only concern is for their deep and immediate loss—the death of their dream of national revival, the death of their hoped-for messiah, the death of their prominence in the coming kingdom. They feared that their three-year campaign is coming to a disgraceful end. Everything they worked for was for nothing. On the streets of Jerusalem heading to the Kidron Valley with Jesus they did not realize then the truth they would later confess, "The Word became flesh and made his dwelling among us. We have seen his glory, the glory of the one and only Son, who came from the Father, full of grace and truth" (John 1:14).

The grief was too much for them. They missed out on the comfort of the big picture of Jesus' coming and goings. The God who comforts seeks to reassure them, but they fail to grasp the meaning of the future Parousia, the fulfillment of the Passion, the gift of the Paraclete, and the promise of his Presence. The disciples were in shock and who can blame them, but we have no excuse for ignoring the big picture. "Would our present lack of interest in Jesus' *now future Coming* (his Final Return) be as disappointing to him now as his disciples' lack of interest in his *then immediate Coming* (his Resurrection)?"[5]

4. Smith, *How (Not) To Be Secular*, 77.

5. Bruner, *John*, 923.

Upper Room Reflection

What might cause you to fall away?

How does Jesus' full disclosure on the cost of discipleship influence you?

Where do you see your faith most vulnerable?

What kind of comfort and encouragement is Jesus giving to his disciples?

DAY 38

The Spirit's Big Work

"But very truly I tell you, it is for your good that I am going away. Unless I go away, the Advocate will not come to you; but if I go, I will send him to you. When he comes, he will prove the world to be in the wrong about sin and righteousness and judgment: about sin, because people do not believe in me; about righteousness, because I am going to the Father, where you can see me no longer; and about judgment, because the prince of this world now stands condemned."

John 16:7–11

JESUS' LITERAL, PHYSICAL DEPARTURE through death, resurrection, and ascension signals a dramatic new turning point in salvation history. "The lifting up of Jesus via his cross to the throne of God brings about the turn of the ages that ushers in the saving sovereignty of God in fullness."[1] The absolute future, that is the future that is absolved of all worldly contingencies, moves forward in the sending and coming of the Paraclete Holy Spirit. The Spirit is not a substitute or replacement for Jesus' bodily presence but the greater fulfillment of Jesus' presence. The real temptation to put someone or something in place of Jesus is in competition with the real provision of the Holy Spirit, who makes the presence of Jesus real in everyone who believes in him, no matter where they live or

---

1. Beasley-Murray, *John*, 280.

what kind of work they do. Jesus, the Man of the Spirit (Isa 11:2; Luke 4:18), is represented by the self-effacing Spirit of truth who makes good on Jesus' promise, "surely I am with you always, to the very end of the age," and "I will not leave you as orphans; I will come to you" (Matt 28:20; John 14:18).

The disciples' grief got in the way of their grasp of Jesus' greater presence. They did not yet understand how Jesus' bodily departure and the coming of the Spirit was about to make possible the worldwide body of Christ. For disciples today, it is not so much the grief over Jesus' departure and separation that hinders God's comfort as it is our inflated self-confidence. We have more in common with the willful ways of the pre-Pentecost Peter than we do with Peter's post-Pentecost humility. The intensity of meaning and the true personal significance of God's real presence is lost when human initiative is valued over divine initiative and self-help strategies compete with the empowering work of the Spirit.

The comforting reason given by Jesus for the coming of the Paraclete is the Spirit's impact on the mission of God. The promise of the Spirit is not to make us feel better about ourselves or to endow us with deeper spiritual intensity. We cannot paraphrase Jesus' promise to read, "When he comes, he will make you successful in the world and help you achieve great things for God." In fact, given the ethos of much of contemporary Christianity, Jesus' description of the work of the Spirit is shockingly negative!

In a deep and profound way the Spirit of truth will prove the world wrong. Wrong about what is wrong with the world. Wrong about what is right in the world. And wrong about who is winning in the world. The Spirit will reveal the shocking truth "that the root wrong in the world is the refusal to believe Jesus."[2] It is almost cool in the eyes of the world to list sex trafficking or drug addiction or gun violence as pressing evils. And make no mistake, these are horrendous evils. But who is going to say that the number one evil of our time (of all time) is the refusal to believe in Jesus? Yet, it is this specific act of evil that is at the root of all other evils.

2. Bruner, *John*, 925.

The Holy Spirit will also prove that Jesus is the best thing going for the world. Of all the things that we might aspire to and
hope for, becoming like Jesus is the most right goal we can imagine. He is humanity's highest hope and greatest good. He alone is
our righteousness. The world's conceptions of righteousness from
the Golden Rule (as the world understands it) to the will to power
fail to recognize that Christ alone is true righteousness and by his
grace he offers us his righteousness. Jesus' simple phrase, "because
I am going to the Father, where you can see me no longer," paves
the way for the full message of the book of Romans. Jesus has made
known the righteousness of God and "this righteousness is given
through faith in Jesus Christ to all who believe" (Rom 3:21–22).
Through the life of Christ, before and after Pentecost, the Spirit
proves that the world is dead wrong about righteousness. No
amount of religious, political, or humanitarian effort can set the
world straight, only the grace of the Lord Jesus Christ.

The Holy Spirit will also prove that the world is under judgment and that the crucified and risen Christ has won the victory
over the prince of this world. As it stands now, the world denies that
there is any kind of judgment at all and affirms that the powers that
rule will always rule. Life is all about present-moment happiness and
living the American dream or the Chinese dream. And when you
die, you die, and after that, nothing. This is what the world wants to
believe, but the Spirit convicts the world that God's final judgment is
real and that our only hope is in the victory of Christ.

The way in which the self-effacing Spirit will convince the
world that it is wrong, wrong about what is wrong in the world,
wrong about what is right in the world, and wrong about the end
of the world, is strikingly similar to the way Jesus went about doing
this in his earthly ministry. Dale Bruner writes, "And in all three
cases, the Paraclete Spirit will do this convicting not by pointing
ecstatically to the Spirit himself or by directing the world or the
Church, sensationally, to signs and wonders, but kerygmatically
(i.e., by the way of testimony, preaching, and teaching), the Spirit,

through the Church, will point exclusively to Jesus himself as the answer to all three of these most disputed questions."[3]

Christian ministries that live in denial of these three fundamental wrongs can expect to be proven wrong by the Holy Spirit. To focus on a humanitarian crisis while strategically avoiding the worst wrong, the greatest good, and the real end, will only serve to undermine the mission of God. Proving the world wrong does not mean that the world will believe in Jesus and claim the righteousness of Christ and rejoice that God has defeated the prince of this world. But in spite of the world, the prosecutorial Advocate makes a convincing and powerful case in the world that the gift of righteousness and the promise of eternal life belongs to those who believe in Jesus Christ.

Upper Room Reflection

What is the number one evil on the Holy Spirit's top ten list of evils?

What is the best thing the world has going for it?

How do your friends expect the world to end? How does the Spirit expect the world to end?

How does the Holy Spirit go about convicting the world of sin and righteousness and judgment?

3. Ibid., 928.

DAY 39

In All Truth

"I have much more to say to you, more than you can bear. But when he, the Spirit of truth, comes, he will guide you into all the truth (or, by means of the whole truth). He will not speak on his own; he will speak only what he hears, and he will tell you what is yet to come. He will glorify me because it is from me that he will receive what he will make known to you. All that belongs to the Father is mine. That is why I said the Spirit will receive from me what he will make known to you."

John 16:12–15

JESUS ENDED HIS TEACHING ministry with much more to say. My sense is that all of us who follow the Lord Jesus feel this way. The responsibility to herald the whole counsel of God is never ending. There is always more to say—much more. The canon of Scripture is complete but our teaching of the Word is always incomplete. We hold to the infallible canon, a finite text in tension with infinite truth. Unlike the Lord Jesus, our capacity even in the Spirit to understand and proclaim the Word is limited—very limited. Like the first disciples we have only a limited capacity to hear and live the gospel message. The fact that Jesus had a whole lot more to say ought to encourage us in the never-ending tasking of understanding, proclaiming, and applying the Word of God.

When I was young I worried about running out of good material to preach, but long ago I learned that no matter how much we teach and preach we will never exhaust the gospel. All of our work is open-ended. Unfinished. We will never be done with studying, interpreting, and applying the Word of God. The biblical text is finite, but the truth of the Word is infinite. This is important, because with the help of the Spirit of truth, we can grasp the Bible's genres, mark salvation history, and begin to comprehend its meaning. Ordinary believers, like you and me, can be shaped and guided by the whole counsel of God. With study and prayer, and the guidance of the Holy Spirit, we can be at home in the biblical text, which is a crucial way for remaining in Jesus. We feel like John when he came to the end of his Gospel. If he were to write down everything Jesus said and did, "the whole world would not have room for the books that would be written" (John 21:25). The wealth of God's truth is unlimited and our responsibility to communicate this truth is unfinished.

Jesus paced his spiritual direction perfectly. He had not run out of time, the disciples had run out of capacity. But Jesus didn't blame the disciples for this. He didn't accuse them of indifference or apathy. He didn't rebuke them. Instead, Jesus comforted them with the promise of the Spirit of truth. "He will guide you by means of the whole truth." There are plenty of instances throughout the Gospels when Jesus accused his audience of stony-hearted resistance, but this was not true of his disciples that night. They were physically and emotionally exhausted. They couldn't take any more in, and Jesus understood their weakness. His sensitivity and empathy is a model for all of us—parents, pastors, and friends, who seek to communicate the truth of Christ. Like our Lord, we have to discern the readiness of those we love for receiving the Word of God. If Jesus trusted in the Spirit of truth to guide the first disciples, shouldn't we trust the Spirit to guide us?

The promise of the Spirit, given first to the original disciples and then passed down to us, assures all of Christ's followers that all that Jesus said and all that he did will be remembered (John 14:26). We are the beneficiaries of the Spirit-inspired biblical canon and the Spirit-empowered apostolic mission. The self-effacing Holy Spirit only heralds what he has heard from Jesus just as the incarnate Son of God only gave what he received from the Father. The perfect harmony of the three-personed God heralds the gospel and brings glory to the Father, Son, and Spirit.

The Spirit not only convicts the world of how wrong it is about what is wrong with the world, but the Spirit also guides the church by means of the whole counsel of God into what is right for the world. "He will not speak on his own; he will speak only what he hears, and he will tell you what is yet to come" (John 16:13). That night on the streets of Jerusalem what was "yet to come" was so much more than the disciples could have possibly imagined. Even though Jesus had promised to rise from the dead, his disciples never expected his bodily resurrection. Nor were they prepared for the outpouring of the Holy Spirit at Pentecost or the heralding of the gospel to the Gentiles. Even after Jesus said "Go and make disciples of all nations" (Matt 28:19), Peter needed a second conversion before he was willing to share the story of salvation with Cornelius. "It was no missionary zeal, and no native liberalism of Peter, which took him to the house of an uncircumcised Roman soldier and placed in the position of having to tell the story of Jesus in that pagan household. It was the Spirit who put him there," writes Lesslie Newbigin, "and it was the Spirit who shattered all of Peter's strongest religious certainties by giving to Cornelius and his household exactly the same experience of deliverance and joy as the apostles themselves had received."[1]

All that the Holy Spirit does is based entirely on the truth that is in Jesus. Jesus says in effect, "He will take you by the hand and guide you into all the truth there is. He won't draw attention to himself, but will make sense out of what is about to happen and, indeed, out of all that I have done and said" (John 16:13, The Message). The Spirit's guidance encompasses the global reach of the gospel, the founding of the church universal, the formation of the biblical canon, the doctrinal development of great gospel truths,

1. Newbigin, *The Light Has Come*, 216.

the confession of the creeds, the social impact of Jesus' kingdom ethic, the perseverance of the saints, and the salt-and-light impact of the gospel.[2] The self-effacing third member of the Trinity comes through in a big way, bringing glory to the Son and to the Father.

Jesus' conversation on the way to Gethsemane challenges us to remain in him—to make our home with him. He is the true vine and the Father is the gardener. And if that were not enough, the God who comforts promises the Paraclete Spirit to come alongside and guide us by means of the whole counsel of God. On Friday he will be "led like a lamb to the slaughter, and as a sheep before its shearers is silent, so he did not open his mouth" (Isa 53:7), but on Thursday evening he devotes himself to comforting his disciples and preparing them for the mission of God.

Upper Room Reflection

How can we begin to embrace the whole counsel of God?

In what sense is the Holy Spirit self-effacing?

How has the Holy Spirit guided you into the truth?

Why might we need a "second conversion" like Peter?

2. Bruner, *John*, 930.

DAY 40

A Little While

"Jesus went on to say, 'In a little while you will see me no more, and then after a little while you will see me.' At this, some of his disciples said to one another, 'What does he mean by saying, 'In a little while you will see me no more, and then after a little while you will see me,' and 'Because I am going to the Father'? They kept asking, 'What does it mean by 'a little while'? We don't understand what he is saying."

"Jesus saw that they wanted to ask him about this, so he said to them, 'Are you asking one another what I meant when I said, 'In a little while you will see me no more, and then after a while you will see me'? Very truly I tell you, you will weep and mourn while the world rejoices. You will grieve, but your grief will turn to joy. A woman giving birth to a child has pain because her time has come; but when her baby is born she forgets the anguish because of her joy that a child is born into the world. So with you: Now is your time of grief, but I will see you again and you will rejoice, and no one will take away your joy."

John 16:14–22

JESUS IS HEADING TO the cross. His "last-minute" spiritual direction is not only necessary in the immediate historical moment, but in every moment ever after. We picture Jesus walking the darkened streets of Jerusalem with a tired and tense band of disciples. They feel the weight of the unfolding drama. Jesus uses the iconic image of the vine to describe the meaning of his abiding presence and costly friendship. He elaborates on new commandment love and refers to his disciples as friends, chosen by him to bear lasting fruit. He warns the disciples that they will be hated by the world and promises that the advocacy of the Spirit of truth who will guide them in all truth.

Throughout this conversation we have been in the company of the eleven, hearing Jesus speak to us as he spoke to them. This discourse continues to reset twenty-one centuries of discipleship according to the revelation of Jesus Christ. We hear Jesus say to us as he said to them, "I have told you this so that my joy may be in you and your joy may be complete" (John 15:11). The Gospel of John has a dual function merging the original horizon with the current demands of the twenty-first century. The divine synergy of the ancient church and the contemporary people of God is worked out by the Spirit of Christ from the pages of the Fourth Gospel.

The Jesus-monologue that takes place after they leave the upper room comes to an abrupt end with a little phrase. The phrase is "in a little while" and it is repeated seven times, four times by Jesus and three times by the disciples. The repetition of this quizzical line especially when read aloud blends humor, confusion, and passion. To picture the disciples "hitting the wall" over this little phrase, "a little while," as if they had gotten everything else Jesus said about loving obedience, lasting fruit, the world's hate, and the convicting power of the Holy Spirit, seems not only ironic but comical. Their silence up to this point may be more of an indication of weariness than understanding, but when Jesus said, "In a little while you will see me no more," their minds began to race. What did Jesus mean by "a little while"?

If Jesus meant that by tomorrow afternoon he would be crucified and that by Sunday morning he would be raised from the dead, why didn't he just come out and say that plainly? Why the ambiguity? And why did John feel the need to devote four verses to these twin sentences with a curious sevenfold repetition of the phrase "in a little while"? The conclusion to be drawn from the repetition and the disciples' consternation is that this is a pivotal moment in Jesus' upper room discourse. Jesus is bringing his message home. The Parousia, the Paraclete, and the Presence all depend on the Passion—the death and resurrection of Jesus Christ.

Our focus has been on the goings and comings of Jesus and the promise of his presence. The God who kneels is the God who comforts by giving the promise of his presence. Only "a little while" separated the eleven disciples from Jesus and his promised resurrection. And only "a little while" separates all believers from the reality of his comforting presence. Jesus' bodily resurrection is pivotal for the Parousia (his final coming), the Paraclete (his gift of the Holy Spirit), and his abiding Presence ("remain in me as I remain in you" [John 15:4]). All four goings and comings of Jesus converge in this pivotal conversation before he prays for his disciples and before he is crucified.

Like the first disciples we may be confused by the phrase in "a little while." Since Christ's ascension we have waited a long time for the Second Coming. Yet, it was only a little while before the disciples experienced the risen Lord Jesus. And it was only a little while before the gift of the Holy Spirit was given. And it was only a little while before the reality of his abiding presence was realized. And it was only a little while before the promise of the Parousia stirred within us a living hope.

In Revelation John identifies the time between the Ascension and the Second Coming as a period of suffering and persecution. This in-between time is represented symbolically in several ways: 42 months, 1,260 days, a time, times, and half a time (Rev 11:2, 3; 12:6, 14). Each reference is to three and half years of persecution, a symbolic duration that cuts the symbolic number of seven in half. Ever since Christ's sacrifice on the cross, the witness of the church has endured the cross. And the Sovereign Lord has determined that the witness of the gospel be given a set duration of 42 months or 1,260 days or three and a half years. This is not "chronos" time, but "kairos" time; not literal time, but God's providential time. The numbers signify a period of grace. The world has been given a window of opportunity to respond to God's mercy, while the people of God live with a keen sense of the immediacy of Christ's coming. They live as if it is only a little while before the Parousia.

Jesus doesn't directly answer the disciples' quandary. Instead, he warns them that they will face great grief in all kinds of trials. He says, "You will weep and mourn while the world rejoices." But then he adds, "You will grieve, but your grief will turn to joy." The transition from grief to joy describes Good Friday sorrow and Easter Sunday joy. It describes our participation in Christ's sufferings and our experience of the power of the resurrection (Phil 3:10). The psalmist's words are true for the contemporary believer: "Those who sow with tears will reap with songs of joy" (Psalm 126:5). Jesus encourages his disciples. Their joy will be greater than their grief. He draws his illustration from the prophet Isaiah: "A woman giving birth to a child has pain because her time (hour) has come; but when her baby is born she forgets her anguish because of her joy that is born into the world" (John 16:21; Isa 26:16–21). The disciples are like this woman in labor: in "a little while" (Isa 26:20) their grief will turn to joy because they have been given "new birth into a living hope through the resurrection of Jesus Christ from the dead and into an inheritance that can never perish, spoil or fade" (1 Pet 1:3). The joy of Easter is so powerful that "no one will take away your joy" (John 16:22), because nothing "will be able to separate us from the love of God that is in Christ Jesus our Lord" (Rom 8:39).

Upper Room Reflection

Why didn't Jesus simply explain what was going to happen from Friday night to Sunday morning?

How is Jesus' bodily resurrection crucial to the promise of his other comings?

How does Easter joy transcend Good Friday sorrow?

What does Jesus' phrase "in a little while" mean to you?

Bibliography

Barth, Karl. *Dogmatics in Outline.* New York: Harper, 1959.

Barth, Markus. *Ephesians.* New York: Doubleday, 1974.

Beasley-Murray, George R. *John: Word Biblical Commentary,* vol 36. Waco, TX: Word, 1987.

Bonhoeffer, Dietrich. *The Cost of Discipleship.* New York: MacMillan,1966.

———. *Life Together.* New York: Harper and Row, 1954.

Bruner, Frederick Dale. *The Churchbook: Matthew,* vol. 1–2. Grand Rapids: Eerdmans, 2004.

———. *The Gospel of John: A Commentary.* Grand Rapids: Eerdmans, 2012.

Bultmann, Rudolf. *Jesus Christ and Mythology.* New York: Scribner, 1958.

———. *The Gospel of John.* Translated by G. R. Beasley-Murray. Philadelphia: Westminster, 1971.

Carson, D. A. *The Gospel According to John.* Grand Rapids: Eerdmans, 1991.

Chambers, Oswald. *My Utmost for His Highest: The Updated Edition in Today's Language.* Edited by James Reimann. Grand Rapids: Discovery House, 1992.

Dreyfus, Hubert, and Sean Dorrance Kelly. *All Things Shining: Reading the Western Classics to Find Meaning in the Secular Age.* New York: Free Press, 2011.

George, Timothy. "Silence and Solidarity." *First Things,* September 9, 2014. http://www.firstthings.com/web-exclusives/2014/09/silence-and-solidarity.

Gladwell, Malcolm. *David and Goliath: Underdogs, Misfits, and the Art of Battling Giants.* New York: Little, Brown and Company, 2013.

Harrison, R. K. *Jeremiah & Lamentations.* Downers Grove, IL: InterVarsity, 1973.

Hughes, R. Kent. *John: That You May Believe.* Wheaton, IL: Crossway, 1999.

Ignatius of Loyola. *The Spiritual Exercises of Ignatius.* New ed. London: Burns, Oats and Washbourne, n.d.

Kierkegaard, Søren. *Attack Upon "Christendom."* Translated by Walter Lowrie. Princeton, NJ: Princeton University Press, 1968.

———. *Works of Love.* New York: Harper & Row, 1962.

Kelly, J. N. D. *Early Christian Doctrines.* San Francisco: Harper, 1978.

Lewis, C. S. *The Four Loves*. New York: Harcourt Brace, 1960.

———. *Mere Christianity*. New York: Collier, 1960.

———. *The Screwtape Letters*. New York: Harper One, 2001.

Litfin, Duane. *Conceiving the Christian College*. Grand Rapids: Eerdmans, 2004.

Luther, Martin. *The Complete Sermons of Martin Luther*, vol. 2. Edited by Eugene F. A. Klug. Grand Rapids: Baker, 2000.

Milne, Bruce. *The Message of John: The Bible Speaks Today*. Downers Grove, IL: InterVarsity, 1993.

Morris, Leon. *The Gospel According to John*. Grand Rapids: Eerdmans, 1971.

Newbigin, Lesslie. *The Gospel in a Pluralist Society*. Grand Rapids: Eerdmans, 1989.

———. *The Light Has Come: An Exposition of the Fourth Gospel*. Grand Rapids: Eerdmans, 1982.

Skinner, David. "In Oprah We Trust." *The Weekly Standard* (July 2000) 22–26.

Smith, James K. A. *How (Not) To Be Secular: Reading Charles Taylor*. Grand Rapids: Eerdmans, 2014.

Temple, William. *Readings in St. John's Gospel*. London: Macmillan, 1959.

Taylor, LaTonya. "The Church of Oprah Winfrey." *Christianity Today* (April 1, 2002) 38–45.

White, R. E. O. "Salvation." In *The Evangelical Dictionary of Theology*, edited Walter A. Elwell, 967–69. Grand Rapids: Baker, 1984.